ALL HANDS ON DECK

FORGOTTEN GREAT LAKES SHIPWRECKS

Wes Oleszewski

Avery Color Studios, Inc.
Gwinn, Michigan

© 2011 Avery Color Studios, Inc.

ISBN: 978-1-892384-60-7

Library of Congress Control Number: 2011905909

First Edition 2011

10   9   8   7   6   5   4   3   2

Published by Avery Color Studios, Inc.
Gwinn, Michigan 49841

Cover photos: top photo by Andy Morrison, bottom photo by
Roger LeLievre, back cover photo by Bob Vincent

TABLE OF CONTENTS

To my cousins Kathy and Dale Hoeppner, who are always there when you need them.

ACKNOWLEDGEMENTS

No author works alone. The time spent hacking away on a computer keyboard and spent shuffling through volumes of information is indeed a solo effort, but the struggle to get that information to the author's desk requires the investment of innumerable people. In the creation of this text I have been lucky enough to be able to lean on many people. I can say proudly that, without exception, every one that I have bothered for assistance has been most helpful and far more than kind.

What follows here is a short listing of those who, without touching my keyboard, helped in the production of this text.

First in the thanks must be D.J. Story, who is my eyes and ears along the Saginaw River. There often have been times when I have been stuck for a fact D.J. is the person that I can count on to find it in the micro film. Also, D.J. always seems to have the time, when I need someone who knows this stuff, to run to obscure places with me and help me dig up lost information. Special thanks to D.J.'s wife, Penny, for putting up with both of us for how many wives will wait patiently on an observation platform at the Soo Locks at 11:30 at night in 38 degree temperatures and nearly gale-force winds while hubby and his boat-nut buddy photograph and videotape a lakeboat? Additional thanks to Don Comtois. When I needed the date that the Third Street Bridge in Bay City collapsed, I asked myself "Who is the one person that I can call who can give me that date right off the bat? Don!" I called him up and after about 10 seconds of flipping through his notes he had not only the date, but the name of the vessel for which the bridge was being opened when it collapsed!

Thanks to Ana (Blodgett) Joslyn who forwarded to me the hand-written account of the Blogett family history, including photos.

Thanks to Walter Lewis who runs the Maritime History of the Great Lakes website. Thanks to my younger brother Craig Oleszewski, who is an Architectural Conservator and Exhibits Specialist and who is one of the experts in overall history that really helps me apply Great Lakes matters to world events. Thanks to my cousin genealogist Kristi Robins who thinks she found "nothing" for me but actually went a long way toward solving a big puzzle. Thanks to Brendon Baillod, a fellow author and research historian, who is one of the best at this detective job of ours. Thanks to Tom Farnquist of the Great Lakes Shipwreck Historical Society, who has put up with on-the-spot phone calls and gives generous and accurate information as well as taking the time to just chat. Thanks to Ralph Roberts who is, in my opinion, the most credible expert on Great Lakes ships - ever.

Finally, the folks of the Great Lakes Historical Society, who have had occasion to bend the rules and let me loose in the stacks. You will be reading the results for years to come. This is just a sampling of the army of dedicated people who struggle daily to preserve and uncover the maritime heritage of the Great Lakes. And thanks to historian Richard Palmer, who has become my connection on Lake Ontario.

Libraries, and those who keep them in order, have been my long-distance research assistants and without their help this book would not have been possible. Thanks to Terry Nandigo of the Flower Memorial Library Genealogy Department in Watertown, New York. Thanks to all of you at the Saginaw

ACKNOWLEDGEMENTS

Public Library, Port Huron Public Library, Oswego Public Library, Grand Haven Public Library, Muskegon County Public Library, Norton Shores Branch and last but not least the Bay City Branch Library.

Finally, my family: my wife Teresa, my daughters Akie and Nattalie. Also, my gratitude to all my in-laws and in-laws to be.

To all of those I have mentioned and any I have overlooked, I thank you.

FOREWORD

THIS book contains historical narratives of true adventures on the Great Lakes. There is no fiction here, no names were changed and no events were concocted. When you read about someone and what happened to them, it is real. You see, there is no reason to make up any drama. The events themselves, as documented in the sources used to recreate the narratives, are exciting and dramatic enough on their own to thrill the reader. There was no need to make up any of the stories, because they tell themselves.

As the author, it has always been my goal to dig up the most obscure stories of Great Lakes adventures and research them to the point where I have discovered every bit of information that I can discover. Then I go looking for more. Indeed nearly everyone knows about the *Edmund Fitzgerald*, and most lakeboat buffs know about the "Great Storm of 1913" because those subjects have been written about many, many times by many other authors. Yet very few know about the adventure of the *Gold Hunter's* crew or the "Great Gale of 1835," which are both contained in these pages.

Additionally, a few years ago, my publisher informed me that my third book, *Ice Water Museum* was going out of print. The desire to preserve two of my favorite stories from that text led to them being included here. They have been, of course, up-dated and greater detail has been added. This is a direct result of having published 11 books in between then and now. I have better sources and resources now, plus over the years a lot of discoveries have been made in the world of Great Lakes shipwrecks. One such discovery took place last summer when in June of 2010 research divers made national news as they found and documented the wreck of the *L.R. Doty* on Lake Michigan. I wrote of that wreck in my very first book way back in 1986 and saw the story published in 1991. Because of that discovery, I have thus re-written my 1986 story after communicating with the team that found the wreck. The updated tale of the *L.R. Doty* is included here.

Above all, it is my job to tell the stories of the obscure events and the forgotten adventures on the lakes and to take you, the reader, there. I seek to place your feet on the deck timbers, to put you on the open lake clinging to a single piece of wreckage amid towering waves of ice water and screaming frigid winds. As you read, you will find your feet walking the lakeshore amid uncut forests as you seek refuge, or perhaps you may find yourself locked in the cell of a waterfront jail in pre-Civil War Oswego. Let these pages be the amazing machine that teleports you through time and space and places you amid the adventures documented here.

THEY WERE WRONG

EVERY year countless tourists flock to the crown jewel of the Great Lakes known as Mackinac Island. They come to see the historic sights, watch the horse drawn carriages and eat the fudge. No motor vehicles are allowed on the island, no real estate is developed on the island and you have to be born there to be buried in the cemetery. It is a unique place that attracts visitors from distant places as well as Great Lakes residents. On September 19, 1996, Sue, a downstate Michigan resident and her husband Walt were making an autumn visit to the island. In their retired years the couple had made regular visits to Upper Michigan and Mackinac Island - mostly for the fudge - but today was different. Today Sue found herself strolling through the island's cemetery looking to tie up an obscure loose end in Great Lakes history.

For a good deal of time, Sue walked among the headstones. The first autumn frost had yet to hit and so the grass was still summer green. She searched and searched, reading each and every headstone, but was still coming up short in her quest. Then, just as she had decided that it was time to gather up her husband and leave, she felt a presence at her shoulder, as if someone had reached out and tugged at her, wanting her to turn around and stay. The feeling was so powerful that she almost expected to find someone there behind her, and she was not disappointed. As Sue turned, she met the very person she had been searching for - a long forgotten lady of the lakes.

In 1887, eleven decades before that meeting, the Great Lakes region was a very different place. There were no super highways and, in fact, there were few roads at all. A few rail

lines were pushing their way into the region, but the best way to get around was on the lakes themselves. Vessels of all sorts crowded the surface of the fresh water seas from the time the winter's ice showed the first hints of releasing its grip until it returned again in December. Every product needed to conduct civilization was transported by boat. Over 2,500 commercial vessels were working the lakes in 1887, and that number did not include tugs and canal boats. The Great Lakes industry was flush with sailors and captains. It was into that market that Captain Larry Higgins suddenly found himself cast.

Captain Higgins had been in command of the lumber hooker *Leland* and was one of the most well known masters on the lakes. After a protracted period of command in the *Leland's* pilothouse, the good captain had the vessel pulled out from under him. Late in the summer of 1887 the *Leland* came under new management and for reasons unknown at the time of this writing, Captain Higgins was not retained as master. In fact, he was not employed at all by the *Leland's* new management. Now, for him, the chances of finding another captain's position mid-season were nearly zero. Larry Higgins, however, was not one to remain "on the beach" very long. He decided to ship out again as soon as possible, even though that would mean doing so as a mate rather than a master.

A forest of masts made up the Chicago waterfront in September of 1887. Walking the dirt flats that made up the loading areas required careful stepping to avoid the horse poop that was left behind by the waterfront's major source of power. Literally, horsepower was what made the waterfront work as they pulled and shoved and hauled every implement of industry. Between the horse pies, the molding hay and the general filth, the waterfront had a smell all its own. But to Captain Higgins that smell was like whiffing perfume.

ALL HANDS ON DECK

Instinctively stepping to keep his boots relatively unsoiled, the good captain sought out friends and former crew members in an effort to find a new job. After just a bit of scouting around the Chicago waterfront he found that a berth for a second mate was open on the Northern Michigan Line's newly chartered steamer *Vernon*. In short order Captain Higgins became Second Mate Higgins and had his feet back aboard the deck timbers of a lakeboat. It did not take long, however, for Captain Higgins to realize he had made a very big mistake.

To the captain, now turned second mate, the *Vernon* herself was relatively unknown, and really was of no concern to him. After all, she was practically a new boat having been constructed just the year before Higgins stepped aboard. Built in the Chicago yard of James P. Smith, the *Vernon* was constructed of wood and measured a modest 158 feet seven inches long and 25 feet five inches in beam. Although some have claimed that she was a narrow vessel, which caused her to ride low in the water, the *Vernon's* beam relative to her length is in keeping with others of her class. The boat's greatest detractor, however, was her bottom's shape. In an effort to make her sleek and fast, her designers had shaped her bottom in a greater crossbeam sheer. That shaping led to her having a draw of 18 feet eight inches, which is more than four feet greater than others in her class. It was an astounding difference that kept her from the short haul, shallow water, small port trade that she was intended for. Instead, plans were made to send her to a deep water career on Lake Superior.

Up on Lake Superior, the *Vernon* had an unlucky rookie season in 1886. Her original owner, Alfred Booth of Chicago, was forced to hasten the *Vernon's* fit out and send her to the upper lakes following the loss of his namesake steamer, the *A. Booth*. On August 27, 1886, the *Booth* hit a submerged

6

boulder off Lake Superior's Grand Portage. The boat later slid off the rock into deep water, sinking, and forcing the *Vernon* to be immediately sent to replace her.

For the remainder of the 1886 season, the *Vernon* crisscrossed Lake Superior taking advantage of the deep water ports and using her handy side-ports for unloading any sort of cargo that could be hauled aboard. Over the winter, while the vessel was in lay-up, Booth contracted with Detroit shipping czar John Pridgeon to have the *Vernon* pull one of his barges between Cleveland and Lake Superior ports through the 1887 season. What seemed like a windfall for Mr. Booth soon turned into a nightmare when the *Vernon* ran her consort aground in upper Lake Huron in June. Pridgeon, who was not the type of person who took such events lightly, not only terminated the contract, but he placed a lien against the *Vernon* for damages caused in the grounding. Booth was left with no choice other than to surrender his one-year-old vessel to the court. In a tap dance of legal and insurance wrangling, Pridgeon bought the *Vernon* from the court for $23,500 and then sold it back to Booth at a profit. In an era when lawyer's fees were on a par with minimum wage, Booth probably felt that he had gotten his boat back at a fair price and could now press on to see a useful career for the *Vernon*. He was wrong.

Shortly after the *Vernon* was returned to service under the Booth flag, the captain turned second mate Larry Higgins came aboard and settled in. Almost immediately, Higgins saw that the *Vernon* had a single and potentially deadly flaw. The flaw was not in her design, or in her engine, or in her hull timbers - the flaw was in her pilothouse. Standing in command of the *Vernon* was Captain George Thorpe and Captain Thorpe was a drunk. In fact, Thorpe was not even a secretive drunk, but was a right out in the open, have a bottle in his uniform coat pocket, hard core all the time drunk. He was abusive, he was stubborn and he even had occasion to drink himself into delirium tremens, a severe form of alcohol withdrawal. Such a condition involves sudden and severe mental or neurological changes including hallucinations. Reportedly, he once went into such a fit while standing in command atop the pilothouse, which must have been interesting for the wheelsman. He also was reported to have routinely left port in a heavily drunken condition and then proceeded to drink more along the way. To 40-year old second mate Higgins, a career captain himself, the antics of this 30-year old first year captain must have been distasteful at best and outrageous at worst. He must have taken some solace in the fact that he normally did not have to stand his watch with Thorpe. The thought probably was that in three months the season would end and he would quite likely get his own command and never have to put up with Thorpe again.

Through the month of September, the *Vernon* sailed and then passed into October. She simply blended into the traffic on Lake Michigan and the Straits of Mackinac landing at assorted small ports and often skipping others because the load on that leg prevented her from entering their shallow waters. Local residents must have been annoyed to expect the *Vernon* and then have her simply steam past or just not appear, but that was a price Mr. Booth was willing to pay.

One series of ports that the *Vernon* was always able to get in and out of were those in the area of Mackinac Island, Mackinaw City and St. Ignace. Unlike the ports along the sandy eastern shore of Lake Michigan, which tended to bar over, the ports in the straits always had plenty of water. On October 27, 1887, the *Vernon* made her now customary stops in the straits. There she unloaded and picked up assorted cargoes and passengers. Among the passengers who purchased passage to Chicago on that trip were two ladies who were residents of Mackinac Island. On their way down to the big city were 29 year old Sallie Durkin and 23-year old Belle "Kate" Gallagher. It was an autumn excursion that both were excited to be taking. As the ladies waved goodbye, the *Vernon* sounded her whistle and Captain Thorpe began drinking. The boat had half a dozen stops to make on the way down to Chicago and Thorpe was no doubt determined to be well oiled.

As the last weekend in October played itself out, a typical autumn gale blew across the lakes. Early reports showed that the lakeboats and crews had not suffered much at all. In fact, one article of the time stated flatly that the month's late blows had produced "…nothing worthy of mentioning." It would soon be proven that they were wrong.

Late Saturday night, vessels passing in the vicinity of Two Rivers, Wisconsin, suddenly found themselves sailing through waves peppered with wreckage and bodies. The lake was still running high and all of the passing vessels found the lake conditions too rough to attempt to recover anything. The captain and crew of the steamer *Superior* saw a raft with several men on it as well as other floating objects with survivors clinging to them. One of the castaways was clearly a woman. Captain Moran of the *Superior* reported that his boat had been partly disabled in the storm with her rudder being wrenched from its tiller by the waves. The steamer had fallen into the sea troughs when they spotted the castaways. Captain Moran had mustered 15 of his crew of 16 below decks in an attempt to rig a temporary steering tackle. The job took nearly three hours and by the time they were able to get the steamer out of the sea troughs, they had drifted far away from the flotsam.

Speculation as to which vessel had foundered began nearly as soon as the reports of the wreckage started. At the ports of Milwaukee, Two Rivers and Manitowoc assorted vessels came in from the stormy lake with building evidence and testimony of a vessel gone down. Into the port of Sheboygan steamed the fishing tug *Welcome* and her catch for the day was the first real lead as to which vessel had been lost. Instead of a cargo of freshly netted fish, the tug had hauled in a life raft with the name *"Vernon"* painted on it. For some that was proof of which vessel had been swallowed by Lake Michigan. Yet, although the tug had also fished out a hat, vest and coat with the raft, some ashore still speculated that the raft may have simply been washed overboard. They were silenced when two sections of the *Vernon's* shattered pilothouse were found 18 miles apart.

There were attempts to notify the local lifesaving stations of the wreck, but where telegraph lines were not blown down, the telegraph stations had already closed due to their

THEY WERE WRONG

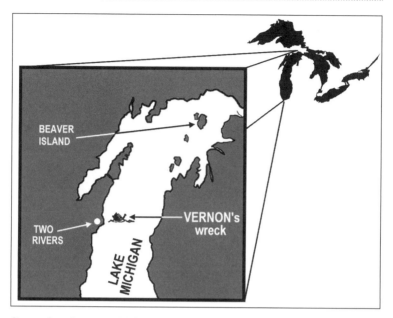

Saturday hours. Although all stations were on the lookout and the standard beach patrols were taking place, the evidence of a disaster was not blowing ashore. Instead, the wreckage field was blowing into mid-lake and out of sight of the lifesavers. In fact, the Lifesaving Service was not even alerted to the disaster until nearly a day after the first wreckage began to appear.

In the days that followed the *Vernon's* wreck, Lake Michigan did her best to keep the crumbs of the feast to herself. The winds blew off shore and the seas ran high, thus keeping the wreckage in mid-lake and making the recovery of any pieces of the lost vessel's remains difficult. Although fishing tugs and passing schooners were able to snag an occasional item or two, for the most part the flotsam simply remained out in the lake. A bitter and intensely cold wind had followed the gale and deterred most passing vessels from altering course to pick up wreckage or bodies. Yet the reports continued to come in of grim sightings in the shipping lanes.

ALL HANDS ON DECK

One vessel reportedly sighted a life raft with 10 people aboard - all "frozen stiff." There were also many reports of the bodies of women floating among the sad stew of the *Vernon's* wreck. Vesselmen around Lake Michigan all concluded that the *Vernon* had gone down and not a soul had survived. Indeed no one could last longer than a very few hours out there among the waves of ice water and the stinging winds of frozen death. Yes, they all agreed, the vessel had gone down and left behind not a living human trace - they were wrong.

Sackcloth black was the pre-dawn of the first day of November, 1887, as the 160-foot schooner *S. B. Pomeroy* shoved into the wreckage field left behind by the *Vernon*. On her way up the western Lake Michigan coast, the 36-year old schooner was under the command of Captain J. M. Comstock. Shortly after four o'clock that Monday morning, the *Pomeroy* began to encounter the wide-spread wreckage and not long after that they saw the first body. At half past the hour, a series of agonizing screams were heard in the distance. All hands were mustered and Captain ordered everyone to listen. The shouts in the darkness continued, yet seemed to come from astern. The schooner was brought about and headed toward the distant cries for help.

All that the little schooner had for illumination were her oil lamps. Holding them as far over the side as each crewman could stretch his arms, their amber glow soon illuminated a life raft with what looked like two dead bodies frozen to its surface. As the *Pomeroy* drew near, a disembodied shout echoed from the direction of the raft. The *Pomeroy's* yawl boat was lowered onto the choppy lake and manned by Captain Comstock, his second mate and a deckhand. They pulled to the raft and as they came near, one of those dead bodies rolled over and got onto his hands and knees. The crewmen had to move fast in order to keep the fear-stricken soul from jumping into the lake. The castaway was not in fear of his rescuers. He was afraid that the *Pomeroy* may sail away and leave him to die.

Two days after the *Pomeroy's* discovery of that castaway, the Fond du Lac Daily Reporter published the following; "Two and twenty mortal relics of the recent lake disaster are disposed on the surface of an earth that was impossible of attainment in life. That which the winds and the waves have reluctantly surrendered may now be allowed a rest denied where nature held its carnival of death. The sole survivor of the *Vernon* wreck, permitted to escape the wrath of the tempest, is the best monument to the remembrance of the perished. The broad blue breast of the ocean seldom is so barren of pity as, in this instance, was the inland sea, salted with the tears of the bereft." The castaway was Axel Stone, the *Vernon's* 23-year old watchman.

Just seven days after the *Vernon's* only survivor was plucked from Lake Michigan's icy grip, a Coroner's Inquest was held to investigate the disaster. There was scant evidence that could be presented. All of the written records had gone down with the boat. No one knew exactly how many souls had been aboard the vessel. No one knew exactly how much cargo was aboard the vessel at the time of her loss. No one knew the names of all of her crew. No one knew the exact time that the wreck happened. No one even knew the exact location of the wreck. It appeared as if the coroner would have a lot more questions than answers. There would, however, be one star witness and one shocking set of evidence. The witness would be Axel Stone and the evidence would be the recovered lifejackets from the *Vernon*.

Axel Stone was a Swede who had immigrated to the Great Lakes region about a year before he met the *Vernon*. As he was sworn in at the inquest, the hopes were high that the circumstances of the *Vernon's* disaster would come to light. Although his English was somewhat broken, Stone clearly made all of his points and set the blame squarely where it belonged - at the bottom of Captain Thorpe's whisky bottle.

At each port that the *Vernon* touched on that last trip, the Captain allowed more and more cargo to be taken on. Through the captain's neglect or by the greed of the boat's clerk, Fred Burke, who was part owner of the Northern Michigan Line, the *Vernon's* hold was crammed with every sort of cargo from pig iron to potatoes. So much cargo was stuffed into her that her sliding side-port doors could not be properly closed. Stone stated that only six inches of freeboard remained when a drunken Captain Thorpe ordered her lines cast off at Frankfort, Michigan, and headed out onto Lake Michigan. So it was that the *Vernon* sailed into the teeth of an autumn storm with what Stone stated was a crew of 25 and a passenger load of an additional 25.

Stone would be on watch until midnight and was witness to a heated exchange between two captains. As the seas grew and the *Vernon* wallowed to the west, Captain Thorpe stood in a drunken stooper, constantly sipping from the handy bottle in his uniform pocket. Below decks, the crew worked at pumping out the seas that were now boarding through the open gangway doors. Captain turned second mate Larry Higgins finally had seen enough. He stormed up to the pilothouse and got nose to nose with Captain Thorpe.

"Sober up you drunken beast and take care of this boat and its people!"

"Go to hell," Thorpe sneered back with alcohol saturated breath.

Toward the end of his watch, Stone could feel that the *Vernon* was mushing beneath his feet and rolling oddly in the seas. He also became concerned about the boat's condition and especially about those open side-ports. He sheepishly asked Thorpe if it would be better to dump some of the cargo so that the side-ports could be closed.

"Go to hell," Thorpe groaned once again.

When his watch ended, Stone retired to his bunk and actually managed to fall asleep. Like most mariners of his era, Stone was in the habit of sleeping fully clothed. Less time spent undressing and dressing equated to more time spent sleeping. Just as he was deep into his slumber, he was awakened by a loud crushing sound that he thought was the crew attempting to launch the lifeboats. There were also the sounds of screaming passengers and shouts that the boat was sinking. Instinctively, Stone opened his cabin window and looked out. In the water, he saw both people and one of the *Vernon's* life rafts. He felt the boat begin to lurch beneath him as he hastily put on his lifejacket and squeezed through his cabin window into the lake.

Hitting the water stung like being hit in the face with a well-packed snowball, only this sting was over every inch of Stone's body. As he surfaced, he saw the life raft and swam to it. Although some published accounts indicate that there were already six people on the raft, Stone is also reported stating that there were seven crewmembers already on the raft. No matter the count - they helped Stone aboard. No sooner did Stone clear his eyes of the lake water than the *Vernon* went to the bottom. Trapped air inside the cabin blew it off the hull and it remained afloat for short time. Stone and his fellow raft passengers saw a few people on the cabin, but the waves quickly broke the structure apart and chewed the people into oblivion. Only one of the *Vernon's* four lifeboats appeared to be launched and the waves soon had their way with it. Stone was positive that as the boat went down, her side gangway doors were wide open. It was a statement that many would doubt for more than 80 years.

Although Axel Stone's lifejacket had served him quite well, many on the *Vernon* were not so lucky. Those were the people who had grabbed the lifejackets marked "Luduc's Tule Life-preservers, 246 Market Street." Upon examination it was found that rather than being filled with cork as would be required by the steamboat inspection office, these lifejackets were filled with sea rushes and other wild seaside grasses. When one of these lifejackets was placed, dry, into a tub of water it water logged and sank in just 15 minutes. Nearly half of the *Vernon's* recovered lifejackets consisted of these death traps.

Sometime near three o'clock in the morning was Stone's best guess as to when the *Vernon* went down. In minutes the bitter wind had benumbed his hands and feet and the unending waves constantly swept the raft. As each wave approached, the heavily burdened life raft did not ride up over it. Instead, it went through the mountain of ice water. With each such submersion, the men aboard were engulfed in a frigid pain only to emerge on the other side and be met by the freezing wind. Hardly a minute went by without another wave and the only time that the wind let up was when the raft's occupants were submerged.

Aboard the raft with Stone was Frank Hall the second engineer, the ship's cook, a coal-passer, two firemen - one of whom went by the name "Bill" and a deckhand. One by one, the cold of Lake Michigan's water began to take them. Although they could see the Manitowoc light in the distance, the icy death invitation of the lake soon became too much. The cook died in what Stone estimated to be about two hours. In short order, one of the waves simply washed his lifeless body away. Within another hour, one of the two firemen was also claimed by the frozen touch of the stormy lady of the lake. At daybreak, the coal-passer stopped moving and was also washed into the lake. Soon time began to blur for Axel Stone as he sat there, too benumbed by the cold to do anything more than watch his shipmates be claimed by Lake Michigan. Sometime later that day the other fireman passed from life into death and, with a wave of ice water, was consumed by the lake. All of these men were simply swallowed by the lake and went away leaving us with no real record of who they actually were. Thus they remain forever nothing more than souls gone to the depths of Lake Michigan.

Mid-morning saw a glimmer of hope turn into deep despair for the men still alive on the raft. Rolling along through the waves came the steamer *Superior*. Stone waved and shouted, but the steamer simply passed by within a half mile of the raft as if no one was aboard the big vessel. The hopes of the castaways were dashed as the steamer vanished into the storm. What Stone and his companions in icy suffering could not know was that the entire crew of that steamer, with the exception of the cook, were deep down in the boat's stern involved in their own life and death struggle with the rudder. As the vessel passed the raft, only the boat's cook was left on watch in the pilothouse.

Shortly after the *Superior* passed the castaways, the one person whose name we do know, second engineer Frank Hall was the next man to succumb to the cold and be swept away into the lake. That left only Stone and "Bill" alive on the raft. They talked while they still had the strength. Bill had come up from New Orleans just a month earlier and signed aboard the *Vernon*. Now he was a long way from the warmth of the Gulf of Mexico's coast and wishing to go back.

Dusk on Saturday brought only frozen torment to the two men on the tiny life raft. It was a torment of lights - lights in the distance that marked the shore and lights passing out on the cold black lake. Amber lamps that marked places where dryness and warmth resided, yet the wicked lady of the lake was keeping out of reach of the benumbed castaways. Her waves danced and played upon their near frozen bodies as she dangled the jewels of salvation in their sight. Through the entire night the two men bobbed on the waterlogged raft never expecting to see daylight again as those accursed lights twinkled.

Sunday's dawn found both men still alive, yet the daylight brought no warmth. The wind was bitter and the seas were still choppy. As if stuck in a frigid limbo, Axel and Bill were too numb to talk very much. Through the day the torment of their situation continued as a steady parade of vessels appeared, passed by and then vanished over the horizon. Some of the vessels came within 330 feet of the castaways and each time Axel Stone would wave and scream, yet none of the boats seemed to notice. It was almost as if the two men on the raft had died along with their shipmates and were now ghosts doomed to forever haunt the cold surface of Lake Michigan. By the time the low hanging sun set, the lake took its toll once again as it sapped the life from Axel Stone's only remaining companion. Bill quietly died and as the night began to hover with all the blackness of a grave, Axel Stone found himself alone.

Lake Michigan was not kind enough to wash Bill's body from the raft. Instead, the lady of the lake left Bill's remains wedged into a depression in the raft, perhaps as reminder of what she had in store for Stone himself. We cannot imagine what Stone's thoughts were as that Sunday night went on and those same amber lights came back to torment him once again. Perhaps he thought that at least now Bill would not have to go through this pain once again. He was now free of such earthly agonies.

Stone's own agony ended with the appearance of the schooner *Pomeroy* on Monday morning - and so it was that he stated that for the record. The members of the Coroner's jury contemplated Stone's testimony and asked a few follow-up questions. Stone's reply detailed that the lower door sections of the gangways were closed, but the upper doors were blocked open by the overload of cargo. When asked about the vessel's freeboard, Stone testified that "...she had an inch and a half freeboard on one side and six inches on the other (side)." The hearings were soon adjourned.

After hearing statements from the *Superior's* master and others involved, a verdict was handed down by the Coroner's jury almost immediately. The jury found that there was insufficient evidence to warrant and censure of the owners of the boat for faulty construction or for the use of worthless life preservers. "But, the captains of the vessels who passed the wreckage were to be severely censured for failing to report at the nearest ports to enable dispatching of relief expedition in time to save some of the person's floating about." This ineffectual jury decision resulted in no vessel master having his certificate revoked or being relieved of command. Even more telling, however, is the jury's total silence on the true cause of the *Vernon's* loss. They failed to make any mention what-so-ever of the boat's drunken master and his insane overloading of the vessel as well as his departure into a storm with his side gangways open.

In the weeks following the Coroner's jury, Axel Stone simply faded into history. His testimony, however, came under fire in the circles of the Great Lakes maritime community. Some questioned if Stone had ever actually been on the *Vernon*. Others openly questioned Stone's ability to judge the vessel's loading. Some speculated that Stone may have some sort of monetary motives is saying what he had told the jury. Many dismissed his statement that the gangways were open. In fact, that argument went on for more than 80 years. In 1969, however, divers found the *Vernon's* wreck and also found that those gangway doors were, in fact, open. Another research enigma turned up in the cases of the two young ladies who departed Mackinac Island aboard the *Vernon* on their big adventure to the big city of Chicago. At least two female bodies were seen among the floating wreckage of the *Vernon* and, in several news releases, Sallie Durkin and Belle "Kate" Gallagher are listed as lost. Yet in other reports they are both listed as "safe" having gotten off the boat on Beaver Island. The records of the identified bodies from the *Vernon* are highly incomplete and of the 50 souls that Axel Stone said were aboard, less than half of those bodies are reported as being recovered. So, how can someone find out for sure if Sallie Durkin and Belle Gallagher actually did get off the *Vernon* before it was lost? They would have little motivation to have done so - this trip to the city of Chicago was a big exciting excursion for the two ladies and no doubt something they had been looking forward to. The way to solve this little mystery is simple - we can let Sallie and Belle tell us… from their graves.

Recall, if you will, where this story began - with that lady named Sue walking through the Mackinac Island Cemetery. Recall as well that only island residents can be buried there and thus, island residents would naturally desire to take advantage of that privilege. Know now that Sue, is my mom and when I ran into this last piece of the puzzle I asked her to go on her next visit to the island and check the cemetery. If either Sallie or Belle are buried there, and their date of death is not 1887, that will be the last piece of the *Vernon* puzzle put into place. Mom told me that she was looking in the cemetery, but found neither lady's resting place. Then, just as she had decided to leave, she took one step in that direction and had the sensation "As if someone put her hand gently on my shoulder to cause me to stop and turn around and look." She turned around and looked down and there, almost at her feet was a headstone inscribed "Mother, Belle Gallagher, 1864-1949." With that, Sue was highly motivated to find Sallie, and in short order she found a second headstone marked "Sallie Durkin Flanagan, Born Feb. 25, 1858 Died Dec. 5, 1933."

So it is that the last piece of the *Vernon's* puzzle is in place, or is it? As with all stories such as this, the more that one digs into the details, the more questions come out. As of this writing, I do not know exactly what caused Sallie Durkin and Belle Gallagher to get off of the *Vernon*. Was their motivation a drunken display by the boat's captain? Were they influenced by the overloading of the vessel? Was their "jumping ship" caused by something said by one of the vessel's crew, or perhaps by the impending storm? These two island natives were likely true ladies of the lakes. Having spent most of their lives getting to and from their island home by boat, they probably knew well the ways of lakes and lakeboats. Thus, even as this chapter ends, the author still has more homework to do in order to answer these questions. Some may have concluded that the questions surrounding the *Vernon* ended with the discovery of her remains... they were wrong.

COPS... IN OSWEGO

AS he walked his beat along the Oswego waterfront, police officer Slatterly found that all was quiet. Indeed, it was a fine spring morning as a fresh breeze was blowing in from off of Lake Ontario and a clear blue morning sky was overhead. The day was Monday, May 21st, 1860, and it was hard to not be in a good mood. Indeed, officer Slatterly's shift appeared to have started off quite well. Of course, like all good police officers, Slatterly knew too well that his day would have much more to do with events happening elsewhere and at any moment the tomfoolery and general stupidity of people would soon break out someplace along his beat as it always did.

Today, Slatterly's work was being started just a short distance away in the office of "Captain" Parker, a local shipping agent. There a supposed sailor by the name of McPherson had come looking for work. Parker enlisted him to go aboard the schooner-barge *W.S. Nelson* which was loading and waiting in the harbor yet short just one crewman. McPherson signed the articles given to him by Parker and was told where to go and meet the boat. What McPherson may not have fully realized when he made his mark on the articles of employment, was that he was now legally bound to going aboard and working on the *Nelson* - like her or not.

Oswego was a very different place in 1860 than it is today. The great fire of 1853 had consumed the wood-framed anthill of buildings and homes that made up the entire northeast side of the city and most of the northeast waterfront. By 1860, much of that side of the city was either reconstructed or being reconstructed. Following the fire, vessel traffic from the lakes and barge traffic from the New York Barge Canal required that Oswego rapidly rebuild as it was one of the hearts of shipping for the entire region. The waterfront was a never ending clutter of masts, sails and wooden vessels of every size and sort and traffic flowed in and around the clock parade that started as soon as the winter ice began to melt and continued until winter's icy grip choked it off once more. In modern times, that bustle of maritime commerce has long ago faded from Oswego and only a few hints of the historic past remain for tourists to enjoy.

So it was that officer Slatterly represented law and order in his little section of the Oswego waterfront. With his boots clomping along the wooden sidewalk, officer Slatterly kept a keen ear and eye out for trouble as he greeted those people he knew along his beat. The waterfront presented all sorts of adventures in law enforcement for the good officer. At the opening of the sailing season he had made a big arrest along with Detective Tremain as they closed a five-year old murder case. The criminal, a man by the name of James H. Clark, had robbed another man by the name of Alvin Curtis at Hall's Saloon. Curtis was beaten and tossed into the Oswego River where he subsequently drown. Over the winter, while Clark was residing in an Auburn brothel, he boasted to an Oswego man about the murder. That man turned the information over to Detective Tremain and when Clark was later spotted in Oswego, the two police officers arrested him. It was quite a feather in Slatterly's cap. Today's big case, however, would not be nearly so glamorous.

By the time newly signed sailor McPherson got to the place where the *Nelson* was waiting, the boat was still loading and not ready to depart. The records do not state just what

COPS... IN OSWEGO

Police officers of old had the same basic job as police officers today, but with a bit more nightstick involved. Although this photo is not of Oswego's officer Slattery, it still illustrates the job and the era. Photo Credit Library of Congress

McPherson's problem was with the vessel, but for some reason he stopped cold and refused to go aboard. The vessel's mate informed McPherson that he had signed aboard and he was now obligated to join the crew. McPherson refused and a very heated argument broke out which caught the attention of officer Slatterly who soon arrived on the scene, nightstick at the ready.

Breach of contract is a matter of civil law rather than criminal law and normally a police officer would do little more than simply inform both sides of that. Yet, being a man of temper, McPherson was already moving far beyond contractual issues and well into the public disturbance area where Slatterly's law enforcement obligation nightstick were best used. Now it did not matter if McPherson did not like the looks of the 5-year old schooner barge, or if he suddenly developed a fear of the water, or even if he had seen rats jumping from her decks and thought she was doomed - he was on a collision course with "I'll show ya' what yer' gonna do" justice. With a well placed whack or two to the melon and a poke to the bread-basket by officer Slatterly's nightstick, McPherson was on his way to jail and the peace was kept once more. Of course, McPherson's signed commitment to the *Nelson* would also be kept. You see, Slatterly informed the vessel's mate that McPherson would only be kept locked up until the *Nelson* was ready to depart. Then Slatterly would bring McPherson right back and plant him aboard the schooner-barge.

For the next several hours, McPherson cooled his heels and nursed the lumps on his head in the dank, lantern lit cell as officer Slatterly continued his patrol. By the time the *Nelson's* towing steamer showed up, the schooner-barge's mate found officer Slatterly and the two of them went to retrieve McPherson from the lock-up with the standard "Now I don't want any trouble from you" warning being issued by the police officer. Like a condemned man, McPherson was marched back to the wharf.

No sooner had officer Slatterly man-handled McPherson back aboard the *Nelson*, than another scrum broke out. This time another crewman by the name of Napier got involved on McPherson's behalf as he physically tried to prevent the *Nelson's* mate from casting off the lines. In short order, fists and elbows were flying as were the curse words. Slatterly moved in again to break things up and Napier attacked him while trying to draw the rest of his shipmates into the fight. Officially, the record says "...and the sailor was rather roughly handled." It is probably a good thing for officer Slatterly that this was about 130 years before every by-

COPS... IN OSWEGO

stander had a video recording device, because Napier was fully subdued and dragged to jail. McPherson, meanwhile, was subdued enough to allow the *Nelson* to depart the dock with him onboard... for the moment, that is.

When officer Slatterly returned from pouring the subdued Napier into the jail cell, he was just in time to witness the *W.S. Nelson* being slowly towed down the Oswego River. He was also just in time to witness McPherson leaping overboard and swimming toward the waterfront. Now, it would not be proper to imply that McPherson was a non-smart person, but it is important to point out that when making his escape attempt, he leaped over Slatterly's side of the boat and swam toward the riverbank where the officer stood waiting. If McPherson had jumped to the other side, he could have easily escaped before Slatterly, or any other officer, could have gotten to him. Instead, officer Slatterly simply grabbed McPherson by the collar and pulled the soaking deserter to the street like a half drown rat. He then escorted him back to the lock-up and, with the splat of drenched clothing on the stone floor, unceremoniously tossed him into the same cell with Napier.

Justice was swift in 1860 and the following day both Napier and McPherson were brought before a judge. No record can be found as to what McPherson stated was his reason for refusing to go aboard the *Nelson*, but whatever it was it must have been enough for the judge to justify his conduct. McPherson was released without additional penalty. Napier, on the other hand, was not so lucky. He was found guilty of "breach of the peace and instigating a riot," each charge of which normally carrying a fine of $100, or if adjusted into 2009 dollars, $2359 each. Often common citizens could not come up with the cash and were required to either serve time in jail or gather up all that they had of cash value and turn it over to the court. At best, we can guess that Napier never again served as a problem for officer Slatterly.

If McPherson had some sort of premonition as to the seaworthiness of the *Nelson* or her fate upon the Great Lakes, he was only off by a year and a half. On October 22, 1861, the *W.S. Nelson* was being towed through a classic autumn gale on upper Lake Huron when her towline parted. In short order, she was blown ashore near Presque Isle, Michigan. Her crew escaped but the 137-foot schooner-barge went to pieces.

THE RITES OF SPRING

Author's note: This story originally appeared in my now out-of-print book Ice Water Museum. *In the 17 years since I originally composed the text, my ability to research and bring out new little details in the story has greatly enhanced. Thus, I have rescued this tale from that book, updated it, corrected some errors and added in some fun and interesting little facts for reprint here. Also, I personally just like this story.*

EVERY year there is a single event that marks winter's passing from the Great Lakes. For some it is the sight of the first robin, or the sounds of free running water in a thawed creek, or perhaps even the start of hockey playoffs. At Sault Saint Marie (the Soo), it is the appearance of the first oreboat of the season at the locks. In modern times, the first boat will crush its way around Mission Point upbound, making the required radio report to Soo Control and the Lock Master, "Up at the Mission." Coast Guard ice breakers assist today's giants as they overcome the frozen Saint Marys River, pushing past the still-closed tour boat docks and the snoozing *Valley Camp* museum ship. Occasionally, a boat from the upper lakes will do the honors, opening the season with downbound cargo. With little fanfare, the first boat of the season will work its way against the floes of pack ice and through the lock. Normally, this scene is acted out in the third week of March. In the year 2009, for example, with the aid of modern radio communications, the "Global Positioning

System" or GPS and the Internet, the whole event was forecast well in advance and little was left to risk. In fact, people could sit at their computers anywhere in the world and watch the opening of the season live from the United States Army Corps of Engineers remote cameras positioned at the Soo Locks, while simultaneously listening to Soo Control, live, by way of the boatnerd.com on-line scanner.

A century earlier, in the spring of 1909, the situation was quite different. The ice had the lakes in its frozen grip until April and powerful ice breakers such as the modern *Mackinaw* had yet to be invented, so the oreboats did not start moving until the end of the month. At the port town of Sault Saint Marie, many of the residents made their living from the fleet of lakers and their crews. Each boat that tied up at the locks, waiting its turn, gave those aboard a chance to go ashore and pick up an item or two that would make life aboard ship a bit more pleasant. When winter closed navigation, the local merchants were left with far fewer patrons than during the season. There would be at least four lean months before the boats and the money that their crews carried would return.

Telegraph information from the lower lakes to the Soo had been hinting that the boats in the lower lakes were breaking out. From Toronto, came word that the Mutual and Merchants Navigation Company's canaller *Haddington* was departing for the Soo, along with the Canadian Lake Lines canaller *J.H. Plummer*. Word from Cleveland said that the Union Steamship Company's 256-foot canal steamer *Glenellah* was on the way up, with the canallers *Beaverton* and *Hamilton*. Additionally, the word was out that Gilchrist's *C.H. Watson* was due at De Tour at any time, along with *C.W. Elphickes* and the 376 foot steel oreboat *G. Watson French*. Like the *French*, the package steamers *Northern Wave* and *Northern*

Light were due in the lower St. Marys River bound from Milwaukee. The lake fleet was stirring to life and the residents and shopkeepers of the Soo could not have heard happier news.

Steel steamers broke ice in those days by way of simply jamming their bows onto the flows and seeing what gave way, the ice or their hull plates. This process of crude ice breaking was commonly referred to as "bucking the ice." On Sunday, April 18, 1909, the *Northern Wave, Northern Light* and *G. Watson French* arrived at De Tour and the following morning all three set out, bucking the ice to the Soo. Through the entire day the three made less than two miles with the *Northern Wave* and *Northern Light* turning back while still within sight of De Tour. The *French* made it as far as four and a half miles to Sweets Point, but that took her until one o'clock in the afternoon. Captain W.W. Eger, master of the *French*, decided at that point that if he were to get back to De Tour before dark, he had best turn where he was and head back. He reckoned that the ice below Lime Island was piled upon itself some 14-inches thick.

Through the evening, the officers of the *French* schemed against the ice and came up with a plan that just might give the boat an advantage. As much ballast as possible would be pumped into the steamers aft tanks, thus lifting her bow nearly out of the water. The big steel steamer would ride up on top of the ice and the boat's own weight would crush a path of open water. Through the night, the ballast pumps worked as the *French's* deck slowly tilted and her fore-shoe literally came out of the water. At dawn on Tuesday, the *French*, sporting her new posture, started once more up the St. Marys. This time she smashed through the ice at Lime Island in less than an hour and by four o'clock in the afternoon, she rounded Mission Point and hauled toward the

ALL HANDS ON DECK

locks. Ashore, expectant residents waved and shouted from the riverbank; the *French* responded with a four-toot whistle salute. Other whistles from the land along the St. Marys rang a responding ditto to the steamer's salute. Soon every piece of equipment whose whistle had steam available, on both the Ontario and Michigan side, was hooting a joyful greeting to the first boat of the season. Crunching up to the north pier of the Poe lock, the *French* was boarded by a happy mob of local vesselmen and dignitaries. Captain Eger was interviewed by the press, greeted by community leaders and, at a quarter to seven in the evening, proceeded through the lock. Behind the *French* came the *Northern Wave* and the *Northern Light*, all of whom snugged up to the wall above the locks and put out lines to await the dawn and their chance to buck the ice to Lake Superior. With less fanfare, four Canadian boats passed upbound during the night and tied up above the locks, highlighting the fact that the Soo was again open for business.

Four days after the *G. Watson French's* triumphant opening of the Soo, the big steamer, along with the *Northern Wave* and the *Northern Light*, was still at the lock wall waiting to proceed. With them, however, were the lakeboats *Superior*, *Sonora*, *Yosemite*, *Sultana*, *Northern King*, *North Wind*, *James S. Dunham*, *Sehuylkill*, *Codorus* and *Rochester*. Waiting below the locks was another fleet of lakers impatient to start the season, the *George N. Nester*, *Superior City*, *William E. Corey*, *Ward Ames*, *Mahoning*, *George F. Baker*, *J.S. Keefe*, *Elbert H. Gary*, *S.N. Parent* and *John Lambert*. On the Canadian side waited the *Midland Prince*, *Midland King*, *Wahcondah*, *Neebing*, *Neepewah*, *Strathcona*, *Westmount*, *Glenmount*, *Fairmount*, *Stormount*, *Glenellah*, *City Of Montreal*, *Advance* and *Scottish Hero*, who had two barges. All were trapped at the Soo by heavy ice that had piled up at

Point Iroquois some 15 steaming miles above the locks, effectively blocking the passage to Lake Superior. Below the locks, the river was relatively clear and the boats had started to pile up at the port. Making matters worse, the steamer *Paliki* was loading rails at the Commercial dock in preparation to head up to Port Arthur and as soon as she cleared, the *Leafield* was going to take her place and do the same. At the same dock, the *Agawa* was unloading coal and would join the crowd when she finished. To add to the traffic jam, there was a score of vessels still coming upbound from the lower lakes with no inkling of the 44-boat blockade at the Soo.

Among the crowd of soon-to-be-stuck upbounders was a rather unremarkable vessel that easily could be overlooked among the snarl of lakeboats struggling to begin the season. Under the command of Captain Robert C. Pringle, the red-hulled steamer *Aurania* sauntered into the lower St. Marys River at dawn on Sunday, April 25, 1909, and headed up to the Soo. Shortly before noon, the *Aurania* pressed around Mission Point. From the lookout tower, the ship reporter shouted via his megaphone that the upper river was blocked by ice but boats could still lock upbound. Captain Pringle responded with a wave of his hand as the *Aurania* continued on her way.

The *Aurania,* herself, although somewhat ordinary by sight, had an interesting background. In 1895, at the Chicago Shipbuilding Company, she originally came out as a steel schooner-barge measuring 364-feet long, 40-feet in beam and 26-feet in depth. Officer's quarters and the pilothouse were stacked upon her spar deck behind her number one hatchway and crew quarters were divided between the standard aft deck house located over her stern and a "dog house" cabin that was set amidships. The *Aurania* sported three elegantly raked spars, one ahead the forward deck house, the second planted

Converted from a barge, the Aurania *retained her square lines. She proved to be no match for the ice off Isle Parisienne in 1909.*

behind the dog house and the third just ahead of the aft quarters. Those spars were an eye-pleasing contrast to her boat's boxy hull. Constructed without the curving sheer of most vessels of her era, the *Aurania* was intended to be little more than a tow barge. This type of construction, known as "straightback" on the three vessels that were actually designed as such, was a passing fad that influenced many vessels built in the mid 1890s. An arresting feature of the *Aurania* was the fact that she had no lifeboat rigging atop her aft deck house. Instead, the two yawls were attached to the ends of the booms that extended from each of her foremost spars. Apparently, it was planned that in case of emergency the life boats could be simply swung over the side and lowered from the boom. Such cost-effective short cuts marked this economy class of lakeboat. Additionally, since barges normally carried a crew that was smaller than the size of a steamer's crew, the smaller and ill-located lifeboats were easily justified by her owners. Interestingly, she was often

THE RITES OF SPRING

referred to as a "schooner-barge" although she was never intended to use sail power of any sort.

At her launching on the last day of August, 1895, the *Aurania* was the largest steel schooner-barge on the lakes. Her primary owner, Chicago Board of Trade mogul W. T. Carrington boasted that the boat could carry 6,000 tons. She was, indeed, an impressive sight that Saturday as Miss Etta Corrigan, daughter of the fleet's owner, made her way toward the vessel while doing her best to remain lady-like and hold her hat upon her head in the nasty wind. Autumn was already stalking the lakes on this the final day of August and the winds were so strong that almost all of the normal gala decorations that usually accompany a vessel's launching did not adorn the *Aurania*. Anything that would have been attached to her rigging or hull would simply have been blown away. With a mighty swing Etta smashed a ceremonial bottle of champagne upon the bow of the *Aurania* and, shortly there after, the vessel slid sideways into the fresh water of the Great Lakes.

Immediately, the *Aurania* began setting new cargo records. In consort with her towing steamer the *Victory*, the *Aurania* hauled down 3,689 gross tons of ore from Duluth to Ashtabula on her first trip. By the end of the 1895 season, the *Aurania* had set the record for a "tow boat" at 4,392 tons of ore. The following season she set the new record for a tow boat at 5,897 tons of ore, which was very close to Mr. Carrington's boast of 6,000 tons. Her owner, John Corrigan, had a real workhorse on his hands and at an unbeatable overhead cost to boot. Tow boats were not required to pass muster under the watchful eyes of the Steamboat Inspector. They required only enough coal to run their donkey boiler and the cook's stove plus they could be manned by less than one third the crew of a steamer. The bottom line seemed unbeatable at the moment.

ALL HANDS ON DECK

Demands for more steamers to feed the industrial revolution, however, soon prompted the *Aurania's* trip to the Detroit Ship Building Company's yard. Just four years after her launching, the boat's career as a schooner-barge was over. The *Aurania* was sent to the yard for conversion to a propeller-driven steamer. All that was altered in the boat's appearance was that the smokestack for her donkey boiler was replaced with a larger funnel appropriate for her new steam engine. Her masts were shifted to clear the way for the newer unloading rigs with the foremast being set behind the forward quarters and the after mast was eliminated altogether. To make room for the additional crew needed to work a steamer, her aft quarters were expanded. Now the new *Aurania* could work on her own or even tow a barge herself if her owners so dictated. Beneath her decks it was a different story as a lot had changed. A triple expansion steam engine with cylinders of 17 inches, 27 and one half inches and 47 inches with a common stroke of 36 inches was installed as her power plant.

To power the engine a pair of two Scotch boilers each measuring 12 feet by 13 and one half feet were also added and fitted with a Howden hot draft system. This system, being a child of the Detroit Dry Dock and Engine Works, was designed to greatly enhance engine efficiency. The Howden consisted of a small steam engine that used a belt to drive a fan. That fan pulled the hot air from out of the engine room and general areas surrounding the boilers. It then fed that air through an area at the base of the boat's exhaust funnel and then through a series of small tubes where the exhaust heat from the boiler added additional heat. The resulting re-heated air was then forced into the bottom of the fire pit and forced up through the burning coal. The system acted as a continuous stoker and caused the coal to burn at a far greater

36

temperature and also to burn more completely. The result was more steam being produced per shovel full of coal. Huge gains in engine efficiency, as well as a far cooler engine room, were the benefits. In mid-May of 1899, the *Aurania* reentered service in her new role as a powered steamship.

When the steamer *Aurania* hissed from the shipyard, many in the lakes maritime community began to scratch their heads and wonder why Mr. Corrigan had taken this huge capacity and low cost oreboat and turned it into a powered vessel. Of course, if they had taken a close look at Mr. Corrigan's figures, those observers would have seen the reasoning. His plan had been to take this simple tow boat and for the trade off of under 900 tons of cargo, turn her into a steamer that could do more than 10 miles per hour with 5,000 tons of cargo aboard. Indeed, on her very first trip, the steamer *Aurania* made the run from Fort Gratiot to Detour, about 225 miles in distance, in 22 and one half hours, and that was against a hefty spring wind and using less than 150 tons of coal fuel. All of this was gotten for a cost to convert the boat reported being between $150,000 and $170,000. Thus, as the *Aurania* sauntered into the lower Saint Marys River that spring morning in 1909, she may not have been much to look at, but she had always been a cash cow for the Corrigan Line.

Shortly after clearing Mission Point, Captain Pringle got a much better idea of the scope of the oreboat blockade near the locks. More than 50 lakers sat with their beams tied one to another waiting for the chance to pass through the ice block upbound. The spring air hung heavy around the brooding lakers with the sooty coal smoke that trickled from their funnels. Through the crowd, the *Aurania* picked her way and nosed into the Poe lock. Passing up at ten minutes after one o'clock in the afternoon, the coal-laden steamer headed past the blockaded fleet and up the river. Some on the waiting vessels scoffed "Wonder where he thinks he's goin'?" Indeed, the ice met her at about Point Aux Pins and with a rumble the shattered frozen surface of the St. Marys River gave way ahead of the *Aurania's* bluff bow. For a while it looked as if Captain Pringle though that he was goin' to Lake Superior, but as the vessels waiting at the Soo knew - the ice would have something to say about that notion.

Unlike the people who managed the lake vessels, the merchants at the Soo were delighted by the oreboat blockade. The town was filled with roaming sailors and the stores, and particularly the saloons, were doing a booming business. It was as if the Soo had been transformed from a hibernating village to a marine boom town overnight. In this, the era before security fences and guards along the locks, people were in the habit of just strolling aboard the tied-up lakeboats. This meant that the moored vessels were a fertile opportunity for every carpet-bagging door-to-door salesman and huckster that could reach the Soo. The result was that the boats were soon crawling with uninvited guests. In response to this problem, the captain of the Steel Trust boat *Superior City* allegedly came up with tasteless but effective solution.

Early Monday morning, Dr. Griffin, the local health officer at the American Soo, started to get visitors asking what to do about the smallpox quarantine that his office had issued. There followed a number of phone calls inquiring as to which boats tied up at the locks Dr. Griffin had quarantined. The news puzzled the good doctor, who had issued no quarantine order and certainly knew nothing about any outbreak of smallpox. By noon Dr. Griffin had heard enough. Scooping up his doctor's satchel and plopping on his derby, he headed to the locks to see for himself. Upon reaching the locks he started asking around, but found that most people had only heard rumors. The arrival of the health officer at the locks now added fuel to the wildfire rumor and it began to spread faster than any infectious disease could. A couple of the lockmen said that they had heard that the *Superior City* had been displaying a smallpox sign for a few hours the previous evening and this bit of information gave the doctor a direction in which to point his investigation. So, armed with that information, he made his way to the upper south pier where the *Superior City* was tied up. Stomping up the wooden rung ladder, the doctor boarded the boat and demanded to speak to the vessel's master. There followed a short and somewhat heated conference in which everyone Dr. Griffin spoke to denied having any knowledge of any smallpox sign. With a stern warning that any misuse of a contagious disease sign would be immediately reported to the Michigan Secretary of State, Dr. Griffin made his way back down the ladder. As the health officer headed toward Portage Avenue, the *Superior City's* captain and mate exchanged a slight smirk. In the ensuing days, there were far fewer uninvited guests aboard any of the boats, especially the *Superior City*.

At first light Tuesday morning the 27th, many of the boats that had been tied up at the Soo cast off their lines and started upbound. There had been little change in the ice conditions at Point Iroquois, but nearly 40 boats departed to attempt passage. The motivation behind such a futile exodus was not a burning desire to load or deliver cargo, nor was it the urge to make money; it was simply the desire of captains and management to outfox labor. The Lake Seamen's Union had widely publicized that their negotiations with the vessel owners affiliated with the Lake Carriers Association were going badly and their 10,000 members could be expected to walk off their boats as part of a general strike before the end of the week. The wily captains knew that it would be much more difficult to "walk off" a lakeboat that was stuck in the ice than one tied to the lock wall. So the boats headed out fully expecting to get stuck less than 15 miles above the Soo.

Ahead of the departing fleet, Captain Pringle and the *Aurania* had already had a rather touchy entanglement with the ice. From Point Aux Pins, the steamer had smashed her way upbound against increasingly rigid ice conditions. As the steamer worked near Bay Mills, the pressure of the floes on the starboard side was clearly increasing and it seemed the *Aurania* was being forced toward shore. After an agonizing struggle, the ice got the better of the steamer and forced the *Aurania* aground. Luckily the boat had only touched the bottom and was not firmly snagged. After a fair amount of swearing and an equal amount of backing and turning, the *Aurania* managed to pull herself free and began once again to shove toward Whitefish Bay.

South of the *Aurania's* struggle, the impatient fleet had also started to do battle with the ice. Unknown to the boats slugging it out on the river that day, a fierce spring gale was charging across Lake Superior at that very moment and was bearing down on the preoccupied lakeboats. A sudden northwest wind erupted and swallowed Whitefish Bay and the Soo whole. Lakes Superior, Michigan and Huron were whipped into a simultaneous frenzy with squalls of snow spitting across the region. Along the lock wall at the Soo the Steel Trust boats, which had been given instructions by the owners not to buck ice this season, put out extra lines and waited, thankful to be in port.

On board the *Aurania*, Captain Pringle had no desire to fight a spring storm and as luck would have it, the winds had blown the ice somewhat southwest, opening the water between him and Isle Parisienne. Without a moment's hesitation he ran his boat for the lower end of the island and the shelter that the islands mass provided. As the *Aurania* seemed within reach of the island, Captain Pringle, Wheelsman William Hocking and Second Mate L.W. Nordeman watched in subdued horror as the wind brought the ice toward the boat once more, this time from both sides. Long before the steamer could reach the lee of Isle Parisienne, the charging ice slammed against her beam and, aided by the wind, shoved her into the other pack. The whole trap, aided by local water currents, started to carry the *Aurania* southeast toward Gros Cap on the Canadian shore. For a while it appeared as if the frozen vise would ground the steamer for a second time. But just as she was approaching dangerous waters, the winds swung around to the east and the frigid clamp holding the *Aurania* opened, again exposing a path toward Isle Parisienne's elusive shelter. Captain Pringle began to work his steamer along the narrow gap toward shelter. Forcing the *Aurania* as far as the ice would allow, the boat's master finally gave up and settled for what shelter he could get. At sunset Wednesday night, the *Aurania* was still several miles short of Isle Parisienne.

Through the night the wind shifted more toward the southeast and crammed the *Aurania* into the thickest of the ice once again, this time just below the island. Captain Pringle sensed the nearing possibility of fetching up on Isle Parisienne. As dawn approached, he resumed his duel with the ice, working as best he could toward the west, but the steel laker came to a grinding stop as her bow crunched into a windrow where the ice had been folded up upon itself making it several times stronger. A series of backing and charging maneuvers were started. At half past seven Thursday morning, she appeared to be working her way free. About that same time, the captain sent First Mate McLaren up to the fore peak to check on the condition of the bow plates under the stress of the ice bucking. The mate reported back that all was in order and the captain ordered another charge at the ice. A moment later the deck beneath their feet lurched as the boat rolled so heavily that for an agonizing moment all aboard thought the *Aurania* was going to keep going and capsize on the spot. Just as suddenly as she started to roll, the motion stopped, leaving the steamer with a severe list. Instinctively, the captain rang full reverse and a long moment later the steamer churned backward in the short channel she had just cut and piled up under full power on the heavy ice at the other end.

After a quick inspection, Chief Engineer Cleveland found an intimidating amount of water coming in below. Exactly from where the leak was coming, he could not tell. Starting the pumps, the chief sent word up to Captain Pringle that the boat had opened her plates somewhere. With that report, Captain Pringle dispatched hands to help in pumping and others of the crew to seek out the leak. For more than an hour the *Aurania's* crew searched frantically, but could not find the source of the intruding water. By nine o'clock that morning, it had become painfully obvious that the water had overtaken the pumps, because the *Aurania* continued to settle steadily. Captain Pringle ordered the boat's whistle continuously blown in a distress signal. There were several big oreboats in the distance and the urgent echoes of the *Aurania's* whistle would doubtless bring them smashing to the rescue through the ice floes.

For the better part of the next hour, the *Aurania* was slowly swallowed by Whitefish Bay as her whistle of distress rolled across the frozen water. But the distant lakeboats that Captain Pringle had been so certain would speed to his rescue just sat there in the distance, like tin cut-outs at a carnival shooting gallery. There were no billows of coal smoke from their tall stacks, no puffs of steam from their whistles and no change in their position at all. Captain Pringle came to a solitary and lonely conclusion there was no help coming. With the *Aurania* groaning and beginning to list even more severely beneath the crew, the boat's master made the decision that every captain avoids thinking about, the decision to abandon the boat.

Abandoning the *Aurania* would have been less complicated on the open lake in a gale of wind. The crew could go over the side, but the lifeboats were designed to be rowed across open water not the frozen surface of the bay. Now they were swung out on the booms and used to drop the crew to the ice. Frenzied feet clopped across the boat's deck as personal possessions were gathered in haste. With what little of their holdings the crew could gather, they started over the side one by one. The thick ice that the boat's stern had piled onto now supported her, allowing a bit of extra time for her people to escape. Departing his charge, Captain Pringle took a final head count. There were 19 including himself; the group was one man short. Conspicuously absent from the crowd on the ice was Chief Engineer Cleveland, apparently still occupied in the lost cause of working the boat's pumps. Mate McLaren was sent below with orders to drag the chief up on deck if need be.

Unknown to the ice-borne refugees, their plight had not gone unnoticed by the distant boats. There were a number of eyes focused on them through binoculars the whole time. From the pilothouse of two downbound submarine deckers, the *George W. Peavey* and *Frederick B. Wells*, the dilemma of the *Aurania's* people was being observed with helpless frustration. On board the *Peavey*, Captain L.C. Boyce was leaning out of the open pilothouse window with his elbows planted firmly on the sill to support the binoculars he had pressed to his eyes for the better part of the last hour. The

From the pilothouse window of the submarine decker George W. Peavey, *Captain Boyce watched helplessly as the crew of the* Aurania *abandoned ship. Locked tightly in the ice near the* Peavey, *Captain Randall did the same from the* Frederick B. Wells, *twin to the* Peavey.

captain had heard the *Aurania's* distress signals loud and clear, but his boat was trapped firmly in the grip of the heavy ice. Now the abrupt ending of the taunting distress signals could mean only one thing; the *Aurania* was at her end. Across the four miles of ice that stretched between the *Peavey* and the *Aurania*, Captain Boyce watched as the stricken crew went over the side. "Blast!" he whispered into the emptiness between the boats as he lowered the binoculars from his face slightly, "They're goin' over now." For just a moment he put himself in the place of the other master, then went back to peering through the lenses like a helpless spectator. The rest of the pilothouse crew stood still and silent with their attention divided between their captain and the distant sinking vessel, wondering what, if anything, the old man was going to do to help. But there was nothing that he could do. His boat was welded into the ice.

Close behind the *Peavey*, Captain Randall of the *Wells* was watching with equal helplessness. Neither of the masters could make out the name of the luckless boat, but her color and profile suggested it was one of the Corrigan fleet and probably the *Aurania*. Her crew now started the imperiled trek across the ice toward safety. Unfortunately for Captain Randall, the flock of castaways was headed away from his boat.

Once Captain Pringle had his crew gathered on the ice, he had a difficult decision that he would now be forced to make. They could head for Isle Parisienne, which was only a few thousand feet to the north, but with the prevailing ice conditions it could be mid-May before anyone could rescue them. In Captain Pringle's mind, no matter how he looked at it, that option could mean a long time eating pigeons and drinking lake water! The only logical path to safety was across the jumble of plate ice to the lakeboats in the distance. Thrown up in tall ridges in some places and split open revealing open water in others, the trip would be a dangerous one at best. To increase their chances, the crew decided to drag both lifeboats and a small skiff, or peggy boat with them. Shoving the two big lifeboats over the first bit of distance and the first ridge or so convinced the castaways that they were simply too heavy a burden. With great relief, the crewmen assigned to lugging the lifeboats left them behind and dragging only the peggy, caught up to the others.

Nearest to the straggling sailors finding a way across the rugged ice was the 524-foot oreboat *J.H. Bartow*, of E.D. Carter's Erie Steamship Company. From the *Bartow's* texas deck her master, Captain White, had been watching the *Aurania's* plight just as his counterparts on the *Peavey* and *Wells*. And just like the others, the *Bartow* was stuck firmly in the ice and all he could do was watch through his binoculars. Shortly, it became evident to Captain White that the group was headed for his boat. This made sense, considering that he was about a half mile closer to the sinking *Aurania* than the other boats. Captain White saw that the approaching men were having a rough go over the ice. In some places the surface was honeycombed and legs would occasionally crunch through past the knee. Plenty of luck would have to come into play if they were to make the *Bartow*.

Captain Pringle's refugees had struggled for two and a half hours before reaching the *Bartow*. As they approached, Captain White had ladders put over the side and the lifeboats swung out and lowered to the ice to help elevate the crew to the deck. In the galley, the *Bartow's* cook had extra coffee and hot soup prepared in large quantities for the *Aurania's* crew when they arrived. While the sailors were boarding the *Bartow*, a chorus of shouts rang from the steamer's rail and multiple fingers pointed in the direction of the *Aurania*. Rolling on her beam, with her spars touching the ice, the red-hulled steamer went to the bottom at half past ten in the morning.

For two and on half hours, the crew of the Aurania *hiked over the ice in an effort to get to the* J.H. Bartow, *seen here on a better day.*

THE RITES OF SPRING

Finally managing to work free of the ice, the *George W. Peavey* arrived at the locks exactly nine hours after the *Aurania* went down. Over the lock wall, Captain Boyce shouted the narrative of the sunken Corrigan boat and the news spread through the Soo almost as quickly as the smallpox rumor. Of course, the facts got fairly twisted. The red-hulled steamer crushed by the ice was reported as a downbounder and the luckless crew were said to have staggered across ten miles of ice to get to safety. As the facts continued to inflate from mouth to ear, the *Peavey* passed through the locks and steamed passively down the St. Marys River. That same day some 44 lakeboats broke free of the bay and headed past Whitefish Point in a grand parade. The blockade was finally broken.

It took more than 42 hours from the time Captain Pringle's boat went under, until the *Bartow* managed to free herself from Whitefish Bay's frigid grip and bring him and his crew to the Canadian Soo. At five o'clock in the morning on the first day of May, 1909, the *Aurania's* crew was unloaded thankfully from their rescue steamer. By chartered tug, the bunch were transported across the river to the American side and gathered at the Murray Hill Hotel for breakfast. Captain Pringle did not waste an expletive in his effort to berate the masters of the two Peavey boats for not coming to his rescue. Little time was left for any counter points of view as the whole group boarded a Cleveland-bound train and headed back to Corrigan territory. With their departure from the Soo, the loss of the *Aurania*, like the winter ice, simply melted away.

For the decades that followed the *Aurania's* sinking, and forever more, the oreboats will crush across the frozen surface of Whitefish Bay to open the season, never giving a thought to the many wrecks that rest below the ice. One in

Cut down by spring ice on Whitefish Bay, the Aurania *sleeps forever, buried in the mud up to her water line and cradled in a trench 430 feet below the surface. Author's Concept*

particular, sitting on the bottom of the bay just off the steamer track, happens to be Captain Pringle's command; the *Aurania*. In 1989, however, an expedition from the Great Lakes Shipwreck Historical Society, led by research diver Tom Farnquist, paid a visit to the ice water museum's *Aurania* gallery. Hovering over the grave site aboard the research vessel *Grayling*, a remote submersible camera was lowered and the boat was found in a trench 430-feet deep, a mile and a half off Isle Parisienne, her deck a jumble of cables, lines and debris. Squatting upright in the mud up to her waterline, the *Aurania* will wait preserved in the darkness for all time. Too deep for divers to reach and too obscure for boat watchers or lake mariners to remember, she is truly a forgotten exhibit.

Exactly why the *Aurania* suddenly sprang a leak and went to the bottom will doubtless never be known, but the cause is likely to be a combination of her touching Iroquois Point and taking an already tender hull in to buck heavy ice. The cause matters little now, as the big boats shove past the forgotten *Aurania*, fighting the spring ice to open each season. There is ore, grain and coal to bring down and little time to think about the boats that had lost their battles with the seasonal ice and now rest deep below in the silent blackness. These are simply the rites of spring at Sault Saint Marie and around the Great Lakes.

AX MEN

AS Lake Huron delivered one more hill of water onto the heels of the schooner *Gold Hunter*, she shuddered and groaned in a frightful manner. But, then again, the *Gold Hunter* always shuddered and groaned in a frightful manner when she was underway in any kind of storm, so her crew paid little attention. With a belly full of iron ore from L'Anse bound for Cleveland she was low in the water but not prone to rolling. The worst thing about this first storm of November was the heavy rain and thick sleet. Although her canvas was an old friend of rain and sleet, the precipitation was so thick that it made seeing where she was headed nearly impossible.

It was likely a combination of the thick weather lowering visibility and the iron ore cargo playing havoc with her compass that drew the *Gold Hunter* off course. At five o'clock in the evening, just as the already gloomy sky was growing into smothering darkness the schooner's crew were suddenly tossed to the deck as the vessel lurched to an unexpected stop. The boat then swung around as her canvas began to whip and flap in the screaming wind. An instant later, Lake Huron sent a massive white-capped wave exploding over the schooner's beam as she heeled over. The *Gold Hunter* had run aground. It was Thursday, the sixth day of November, 1879, and although they may have suspected it, no one aboard the little boat knew that the 23-year old schooner had found her final resting place.

Although the records are silent on what followed immediately after the stranding, logic tells us that her crew probably remained aboard her for some time. What the records do tell us is that her hull was holding up nicely against the breaking seas, so there was little point in launching the *Gold Hunter's* single lifeboat and abandoning the ship. Darkness was rapidly setting in and in the rough seas, the lifeboat was more likely to dump and drown its passengers than it was to get them ashore. The odds are that everyone remained aboard and simply secured the lifeboat from being swept away and worked at keeping themselves more protected from the storm.

Dawn the following day presented extremely cold weather, but the winds and the waves had faded to the point where the schooner's boat could easily be launched. As best can be gleaned from records, that lifeboat contained just four of the 135-foot long schooner's crew of eight. Arthur Baker, John Baptist, Arthur Johnson and John Cox were aboard the tiny yawl as it was launched and rowed toward the Michigan shore. The mission of the occupants of the little boat was to simply go ashore and try and find a way to get help for the schooner. At this point, none of the *Gold Hunter's* crew really knew exactly where they were, but just before dawn a lighthouse's flashing beacon could be seen on the horizon to the south. If the crew were unable to find anyone ashore, they could likely hike the distance to the lighthouse.

Carrying extra clothing and some scant provisions, the four castaways landed on the sandy shore of mainland Michigan. It was easy to see that their schooner had run into the southeast end of a long thin island that ran east and west. The shore was thickly forested with tall pine and there was no sign of civilization in the immediate area as they beached their lifeboat. Trekking into the woods, the four mariners

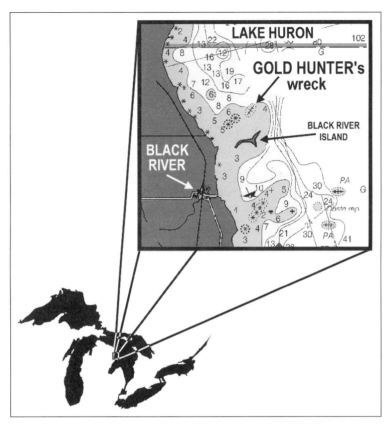

suddenly came upon what should have been their salvation. It was rustic shanty, but there was smoke coming from the stovepipe and that could only mean that there must be warmth and people inside. As they approached the shack they were sure they had been saved but in fact, they would have been better off if they had remained on the wreck.

What greeted the castaways was not a sympathetic group of local residents at all. Instead they stumbled into a nest of lumberjacks with very sharp axes and very ill intent. Under threat of the blades of the lumber cutter's axes, the entire shore party was robbed of every possession that they had from money, food and tobacco to the extra clothing that they carried. Then they were run off into the woods by the ax brandishing lumberjacks, but not before one member of the crew had the coat stolen from off his back and his hat stolen from his head.

The odds are that the startled castaways regrouped following their mugging by the ax men and then headed back to the beach and south toward the lighthouse still unaware of their actual location. It would be a long cold hike, but one thing was for sure, they could not go backward to where they had landed. The thugs with the sharp axes had made it clear that if they returned they would suffer worse than simple robbery. Besides, it was a good bet that the ax men would soon steal their lifeboat as well.

There was really no law in the area where the crew of the *Gold Hunter* had landed. The nearest sheriff was over 80 miles away. The fact that some thugs out in the woods had threatened the four mariners with axes and stolen their possessions really meant nothing in terms of where they were. Yet, in fact, they had not landed in a simple wilderness at all, but they had actually come ashore on private property which belonged to a man who would one day become the Governor of Michigan. The *Gold Hunter* had fetched up on the southeast bar of the pork chop bone shaped Black River Island just a few yards off shore from lumber baron Russell Alger's stake of 100 square miles of pine forest. It is likely that the ax men who mugged the crew were in Alger's employ.

In this era of king lumber, the logging companies could care less about a wood-cutter's background or even his name for that matter. All that was important was the fact that he was able to swing an ax every day through the entire winter. For that reason alone, the up-state lumber camps were a good place for down-state criminals to hide in plain sight. Although not all lumberjacks were criminals, it is easy to see how a bunch of hoodlums could group together in a single lumber shanty.

What the four cold mugging victims could also not know as they set out toward the lighthouse, was that in about a mile they would come upon the mouth of Black River and the settlement by the same name that was quickly growing thanks to Mr. Alger's lumber business. There it is likely that they came into contact with the person who, in that era, was the hub of all of the town's activity. It was not the sheriff or the mayor or even Mr. Alger, in 1879, the anchor of any small village was the local postmaster and in Black River, that person was Edgar O. Cheney. It is also most likely that with the help of Postmaster Cheney the castaways were able to get the word out as to the *Gold Hunter's* location and the schooner's situation.

Word of the *Gold Hunter's* stranding would have to have been sent by courier to the lighthouse and life-saving station at Sturgeon Point, 10 miles to the south of Black River Island. A courier would be needed because telegraph lines to the Sturgeon Point station would not even be established for another 20 years. So, on the morning of November 8th, the life-savers were alerted to the vessel and they immediately launched their surfboat and headed to the scene. What they found was not a disaster but a calm captain and crew who informed them that no rescue was needed. In fact, word had already been sent and a tug had been chartered to come to the scene with steam pumps to aid in getting the *Gold Hunter* refloated. The life-savers were also informed that the entire crew wanted to remain aboard the boat while waiting for the tug. That was their choice, but the life-savers instructed the *Gold Hunter's* captain to fly his flag at half mast if he needed additional assistance. An eye would be kept upon the stranded schooner from the Sturgeon Point lighthouse tower by the life-savers. With that arrangement agreed upon, the storm warriors rowed back to their station.

Within a day the tug *Forest City* came chugging onto the scene and the steam pumps were rigged and running. As the ore-stained red water was siphoned overboard into Lake Huron's glassy depths, everyone was confident that soon the *Gold Hunter* would be pulled clear of the shoal. But the lake had other ideas. As swiftly as the first storm had died, another and far more powerful storm blew up. This time the bigger and more violent ice water seas beat upon the *Gold Hunter's* wooden hull until she began to come apart. The boat's crew had no choice; they were forced to flee to the tug as the schooner rapidly went to pieces. Sailing off into the gale, they even left the steam pumps behind, deciding it was better to come back and recover them later. Of course, there was no way that any of them were going ashore, not in that location. They liked the clothes on their backs too much to face the ax men in the woods again.

Today the beach where the crew of the *Gold Hunter* made landfall is dotted with some fine lakefront homes and cabins. Ridge Road, as it runs east and west from the lakefront to Lake Shore Drive, approximates the route that the castaways would have taken as they came upon the evil ax men. So if you happen to be up that way, perhaps looking to visit nearby Newegon State Park, it may be fun to stop and take a stroll back in time. Just take care not to violate any private property and not to run into any ax men.

SOMETIMES YOU JUST HAVE TO WAIT YOUR TURN

SUNDAY the fifth day of June, 1887, should have started out with a pleasant summer sunrise at Milwaukee, Wisconsin, but it did not. Instead, the church bells were muffled by a thick fog that extended far out into Lake Michigan. Standing in the lookout turret atop the Milwaukee life-saving station, the surfman on watch kept a keen ear toward the lake. Ears were his only tool because as far as the use of his eyesight was concerned, it was a pointless activity. The fog was so thick he may as well have had a bed sheet over his head. Still, he sensed that trouble was out there in the mist. He could almost smell it as each soft breeze that came in from the lake seemed to be scented with the smell of wet timbers. Indeed, in weather like this, trouble was out there, someplace. He simply had to stay alert and wait his turn to go into action.

Later in the day, the fog inland had lifted, but a thick haze still lingered over the lake. It was then that a little old man in a small rowboat was spotted, pulling his way off the lake into the inner harbor and toward the life-saving station. With a bit of rumpled resignation, the man from the rowboat dragged the craft up out of the water and then proceeded up to the station's door and firmly knocked. When Station Keeper Peterson answered the door he instantly recognized the man as Captain Nelson, master of a Milwaukee based scow-schooner the *Black Hawk*. He had come calling at the life-saving station in order to report that his vessel had gone aground in the fog. The boat was located just four miles above the station at a spot

ALL HANDS ON DECK

Captain Mabee of the steamer George Burnham *was willing to wait his turn as he sent the life-savers to tend to the wounded schooner* Johnson *rather than having them work his boat. Photo Credit Ralph Roberts collection*

known locally as "North Point." Captain Nelson made it clear that his boat was in no immediate danger, but considering that he had only a crew of four, he was going to need some help running lines to get her free. Of course the life-savers were only too happy to spring into action. You see, one of the ways that the United States Life-Saving Service justified their budget to the Congress was not only by the lives that they saved, but also by an annual tally of the value of property they saved. So, as Captain Nelson trudged into town to charter a tug, the Milwaukee life-savers launched their surfboat and pulled toward North Point.

Scow-schooners were not unique to the Great Lakes. In fact they have been used all over the world. One of the last operational scow-schooners can be found, as of this writing, floating at the San Francisco waterfront. Still, scow-schooners were popular on the lakes for the same reason as they were popular elsewhere - because they could be very heavily loaded and still remain stable plus sail in very shallow waters. Their flat bottoms and boxy hulls were perfect for winding waterways and shallow inlets. Most had a retractable centerboard that enhanced their stability and all of them could be manned with about half the crew of a standard schooner. When the surfmen arrived on the scene, they found the little 172-ton *Black Hawk* stuck firmly on the shoal and loaded to the hilt with lumber.

No sooner had the storm warriors come alongside than they got to work on the stranded *Black Hawk*. While some of the surfmen took to the boat's hand operated bilge pump, others began tossing her deck-load of lumber overboard while others recovered and rafted the timbers together. About an hour after the life-savers arrived, the tug out of Milwaukee arrived with Captain Nelson. By late evening, the life-savers had removed between 30,000 and 40,000 board-feet of lumber from the deck of the *Black Hawk*. It was not her full load, but it was enough to refloat her. The big issue then was that the boat had a bad leak. Apparently, as she ran ashore she had struck a boulder head-on and split her forefoot. Constant pumping at her bilge pump would keep her from sinking, but not by much. The life-savers would have to remain aboard and pump in shifts until the tug could get her into Milwaukee. There steam pumps could be put aboard and keep her afloat until her forefoot could be repaired.

With blistered hands and bent backs, the life-savers stood triumphantly on the decks of the *Black Hawk* as the tug towed her into the protection of Milwaukee harbor. No one ashore took much notice, however, because the arrival took place at ten o'clock at night. Still, the life-savers had to feel that they had accomplished a good day's work when it was their turn to go to the rescue. They had no idea that their work was only beginning.

Nearly a dozen miles north of where the *Black Hawk* had run ashore, Captain D.W. Matteson of the schooner-barge

C.N. Johnson stood on deck awaiting the help of the life-savers. His boat had been in tow of the 160-foot wooden steamer *George Burnham* out of Sandusky, Ohio, with a load of coal when they ran into the fog and then collided with the state of Wisconsin. Once the fog lifted, a careful look to the south saw another vessel's silhouette ashore in the distance. From Captain Matteson's viewpoint, he was at least number three in line to be rescued. He was simply going to have to wait his turn in line, a situation that all mariners are more than familiar with.

Word of the additional stranded lakeboats reached the life-savers as soon as they began securing the *Black Hawk* in Milwaukee harbor. They immediately boarded the tug that had towed the *Black Hawk* in and headed out toward the reported location of the vessels in distress. Just before one o'clock in the morning, the dim amber lamps of a schooner came into view of the tug and the life-savers. She was the 140-foot laker *Quickstep*, formerly the *S. Anderson*, and she was loaded with lumber from Muskegon, Michigan.

Captain Becker of the *Quickstep* had fallen prey to the fog just like Captain Nelson of the *Black Hawk*. The only difference was that the *Quickstep* was not a scow-hull and she had really shoved herself into the bar. The records say that in order to release her from the shallows, it was "…necessary for the tug to dredge out a channel…" It is not stated exactly how that was done, but there are areas in Lake Michigan's Whitefish Bay where the bottom is heavily sanded. If one of these was where the *Quickstep* had fetched up, the tug's propeller may have been used. Still, this was a risky venture considering that it was being done at night and a single bolder or submerged log lodged in the sand could easily have knocked the tug out of action.

By the time that daylight broke across Lake Michigan, the *Quickstep* was free of the shallows and setting sail for

SOMETIMES YOU JUST HAVE TO WAIT YOUR TURN

Milwaukee. Now the life-savers set their sights on the steamer aground at Fox Point some four miles farther north. Sitting quietly with her nose in the sand was the steamer *Burnham*. A trickle of smoke was coming from her smokestack as she waited for assistance. As the tug with the life-savers approached the *Burnham* her master, Captain Mabee, indicated that his boat could wait. He felt sure that the *Johnson* appeared to be in far worse condition. Two tugs were already working the *Johnson* and not making a sliver of progress, so the life-savers headed off to lend some extra, but blistered hands.

Captain Mabee was quite correct in his evaluation concerning the condition of the *Johnson*. Her 31-year old hull had not taken her run onto the shoal well. She was leaking badly and all of the pulling in the world was not going to get

As of this writing, no photos of the Black Hawk *have been located. She would have closely resembled this unidentified scow-schooner, however. Photo Credit Ralph Roberts collection*

her moved. Her six crewmen were already exhausted from pumping and now tons of coal needed to be shoveled out of her hold and dumped into the lake in order to lighten her. Each tug on the scene had only enough men aboard to handle the tug's operations. Normally that was no more than the captain, an engineer and a one deck hand to handle the lines. The extra man-power provided by the life-savers made all of the difference. They immediately went at her pumps and then took turns shoveling coal overboard. The work was hot and sweaty and the sleepless life-savers went about the chore like zombies. The only good thing was that the biting flies had yet to come out for the season on Lake Michigan.

After several hours of pumping, shoveling and the combined pulling by all three tugs, the *Johnson* was pulled free of the shoal. Captain Matterson, however, was far from being relieved. His boat was still leaking badly and if the hand pumps could not keep up their pace, she could very well settle to the bottom once again, only this time it would be in deep water. Somewhat to his dismay, the life-savers and the small fleet of three tugs now would have to head for the *Burnham*. Captain Matterson would have to wait, again, for his turn to be towed into the safety of Milwaukee harbor.

Aboard the *Burnham*, Captain Mabee was not about to have one single dime of his cargo tossed into Lake Michigan - no sir. Still, the steamer had to be lightened if she was to be pulled off, and there was no time to waste, the *Johnson* was standing in deep water and leaking. Quickly a compromise was reached. The life-savers would shovel the coal needed to lighten the *Burnham* overboard onto the decks of the three tugs. Once the tugs had all they could hold, if any additional coal needed to be jettisoned, it would go into the lake. Officially, it is estimated that the life-savers shoveled, wheel barrowed and dumped about 20 tons of coal out of the

Burnham and onto the tugs. A bit of hard pulling by the three tugs hauled the steamer free and she was able to move back to the *Johnson*. There the life-savers re-boarded the schooner-barge and went back to work at pumps.

All the way into the harbor of Milwaukee the life-savers pumped at the *Johnson* and kept her afloat. By the time they got to the dock, shore crews took over from the exhausted surfmen who returned to their station. In all, the life-savers had been at work unloading, pumping, shoveling and running lines for more than 24 hours straight. When they returned to the station, the keeper sat down and was able to log $59,470 in property saved as well as 31 lives. You see, technically, by USLSS rules, if you were on the boat in distress when the life-savers reached you and you made it to shore with their help, they saved your life. At least, that's the way it was tallied at the end of each fiscal year. As the keeper, Peterson, added up and logged the values and lives, his surfmen went to bed, all except for one. You see, even though they had been awake and working hard for more than 24 hours, the USLSS rules also said that one of the surfmen still needed to go atop the station and stand a long watch in the lookout turret because it was his turn.

LITTLE LADY OF THE LAKES

Author's Note: When researching shipwrecks and other maritime events in history, it is rare to stumble across any recorded event that does not involve death and tragedy. However, when such an event is found, one that involves joy, goodness and fine tradition, it has to be recorded in the history book. The following joyful event was found when I was doing my daily visit to the news section of the boatnerd.com web site. It made me instantly happy and I knew it would do the same for my readers. Thus, I here depart from the mayhem of shipwrecks and disasters and take you, the reader, in a different direction for a moment.

WINTER was grudgingly releasing its grip on the upper Great Lakes on the 8th day of May 2010. At Sault Saint Marie, Michigan, snow was still falling as the Coast Guard Cutter *Mackinaw* sat moored to the Carbide Dock. In the pilothouse of the *Mackinaw* members of her crew stood ramrod straight and garbed in the finest dress uniforms. A gathering of civilian guests were also in attendance, dressed in their Sunday best outfits. They were there to be witness to a very special event; an event of pride, an event of tradition and an event that had never before taken place upon the decks of this vessel. Resting in a specially constructed stool-like holder was the ship's bell. Crewmembers of the *Mackinaw* had removed the bell from its normal mountings and spent a good deal of time and elbow grease polishing it to a mirror glaze. Not a fingerprint would be found on it today, not even with a microscope. Theirs was not a labor of duty in polishing the bell, rather it was a labor of pride, joy and love. This preparation of the *Mackinaw's* bell was also not an effort to greet a head of state or a Coast Guard officer of extreme rank. It was in honor of what many of the crew considered to be the most important person ever to come aboard the vessel; a tiny, squirming, bundle of absolute joy known best aboard the *Mackinaw* as baby "Poe."

Under the watchful eye of Commander Scott J. Smith, the *Mackinaw's* captain, the party of crew and guests prepared to witness an old tradition aboard naval and Coast Guard vessels. That tradition is the christening of a child using the ship's bell. This had been requested by the parents of this new little lady of the lakes. Her father, Lieutenant Cory D. Cichoracki is an officer aboard the *Mackinaw* and at the family's request, the vessel's commander granted his permission to go ahead with the ceremony. On hand to carry out the honors was United States Navy Chaplain, Lieutenant Commander Jeffrey Plummer.

For Lieutenant Cichoracki most of the past year had been spent aboard the *Mackinaw* with the constant thought of his expectant wife Margaret and their unborn child always in the back of his mind. But he was not alone in that thinking. Soon the whole crew of the *Mackinaw* had the expected baby on their minds. Although all ships in the service of the United States have crews that take on the characteristics of a family, vessels and stations of the Coast Guard are especially tight knit. When one member of the crew is expecting, the whole crew is expecting. Before long, the entire crew of the *Mackinaw* were experiencing the all-overs of parents to be. The upcoming member of the Cichoracki family was soon a familiar subject of talk around the ship. There was just one problem - no one knew if it was to be a boy or a girl, so no one knew what to call it.

Although modern Ultrasound technology allows parents to discover the gender of their expected child very early on in the pregnancy, and several such examinations are done routinely prior to birth, many parents elect not to know. Not knowing allows for a bit more fun on the date of birth and that was the route that Lieutenant Cichoracki and his wife decided to take. Unfortunately, the members of the *Mackinaw's* crew really found it hard to keep referring to the baby as "it." Indeed a nick-name needed to be invented.

It was the *Mackinaw's* Executive Officer who inadvertently came up with the expected baby's nick-name. You see, schedules for many events around the lakes are published far in advance and so the crew of the *Mackinaw* knew pretty well where they would be and when they would be there. Coincidentally, it turned out that the scheduled date for the biggest event of the season for any icebreaker, the 2010 opening of the locks at the Soo, was the same as the baby's due-date of March 25th. Since the Poe Lock is the first lock to annually come into service, and the *Mackinaw* and her sister icebreakers center their passages through that lock, the ship's exec. suggested that they should call "it" baby "Poe Lock." This was also a side-handed joke eluding to Lieutenant Cichoracki's Polish heritage. Of course those of us who are of a Polish heritage are well equipped with a hearty sense of humor and Lieutenant Cichoracki took the suggestion as being all in fun. Oddly, however, part of the nick-name stuck and soon the baby that everyone aboard the *Mackinaw* was expecting, began to be referred to fondly as baby "Poe." This nick-name worked well, because it would fit either a boy or a girl.

As the calendar turned from 2009 to 2010, Baby Poe's due-date loomed as large in the future of the *Mackinaw's* crew as

ALL HANDS ON DECK

Prevented from docking by heavy winds, the powerful Mackinaw
*hovers off its namesake city. Aboard the big cutter when this photo
was taken is the littlest lady of the lakes.* Photo Credit Dianne Donati

did the annual break-out of the first lake freighters. Little Poe
was going to arrive at the very peak of ice-breaking season.
The problem was that in the Coast Guard, as in all of the
services, duty comes ahead of everything. Lieutenant
Cichoracki knew that very well. He had enlisted in the Coast
Guard in 1991 and spent a dozen years as a Quartermaster
before being selected for Officer Candidate School and then
returning to service as an officer. Fortunately, he was now
given the permission of Commander Scott to carefully
coordinate his schedule aboard the *Mackinaw* with a good
friend and former shipmate on the vessel. She was able to
move from her unit to the *Mackinaw* in order to allow
Lieutenant Cichoracki to be home for the birth of Baby Poe.

On the big day, Lieutenant Cichoracki was there when
Baby Poe arrived and one of the first things he did was to

contact the crew of the *Mackinaw* and give them the good news. The baby was a beautiful little girl and her name would be Isabella. By pure coincidence, at that same time the *Mackinaw* just happened to be in the Poe Lock.

Lieutenant Cichoracki had learned of the tradition of christening a baby with the ship's bell early in his career with the Coast Guard. It is a naval tradition that dates back more than two centuries and is said to have originated with British Royal Navy. The bell christening ceremony was adopted long ago into the Canadian Navy, the United States Navy and later the United States Coast Guard. As a part of the tradition, the person who has been christened also gets their name engraved inside the bell and some sources say that at the time that the vessel is decommissioned, that person is awarded the bell itself. That awarding of the bell portion of the tradition is said to no longer be followed. Still, when Lieutenant Cichoracki checked into it, he discovered to his surprise that a bell christening had never been done aboard the *Mackinaw*.

Although the parents of the newest lady of the lakes were excited about the idea of doing a bell christening aboard the *Mackinaw*, they had to take somewhat of a second place to the vessel's commanding officer. Commander Smith was highly excited about the christening and in short order the entire crew were energized over the idea. This would likely be the most joyful day aboard the vessel since her launching on the second day of April, 2005.

The date for the christening was set so that the ceremony could take place while the *Mackinaw* was underway returning to Cheboygan from the Mackinaw City maritime festival. Baby Poe and her parents boarded the *Mackinaw* in Cheboygan and headed up the lake. Awaiting them in Mackinaw City were the chaplain and the family members who were there to witness the event. As often happens,

Tied up just below the locks at Sault Saint Marie, the Coast Guard cutter Mackinaw *poses proudly. As this photo was taken, baby "Poe" was being Christened in a long standing tradition of honor and joy.* Photo Credit Lee Rowe

however, the Great Lakes had other ideas as to where and when Baby Poe would be christened. As the *Mackinaw* headed toward the port of that same name, Lake Huron stirred up a nasty bit of weather. So bad were the conditions that the big Coast Guard vessel could not tie up. To make matters worse, the weather was also too nasty to permit the *Mackinaw* to return to Cheboygan. The winds had come up so strong that the laker *Atlantic Huron* was blown from the Detroit River's channel and grounded. In such a blow, the *Mackinaw's* best bet was to head for the Soo. Thus Commander Scott ordered her headed into the shelter of the Saint Marys River and up to Sault Saint Marie. Luckily for the guests who were waiting ashore in Mackinaw City, the trip to the Soo by car is only an hour long drive. Still, coordinating the logistics for the whole shift in plans must have been a bit of a nightmare. Perhaps this was just the Great Lakes saying that they thought this christening of this new lady of the lakes needed to be done at the Soo.

On that snowy morning at Sault Saint Marie Baby Poe was baptized over the up-turned bell of the powerful ice-breaker *Mackinaw*, much to the joy of everyone. In the days that followed, the *Mackinaw* returned to her home port of Cheboygan. Commander Smith took the ship's bell and headed down Main Street to the Mary Ann Archer Jewelry store. There he had the jeweler do the final honor of inscribing the baby's name inside the bell. Another part of the bell christening tradition says that the inscription will bring good luck to the boat. Today, as you read this, the *Mackinaw* is hard at work someplace on the Great Lakes and on her bell is inscribed the name Isabella Cichoracki and the words "Poe," Christened May 8, 2010. It is a fitting tribute to a true little lady of the lakes.

ALONG PRIDGEON'S LINE

Author's note: In 1992, I wrote the story seen here for my third book Ice Water Museum. *Since then I've researched and written 11 more books. As time went by, my capability and ability to research as well as my sources became exponentially better. Then, in 2007, the publisher informed me that* Ice Water Museum *was going out of print. I knew that this was my chance to update this story with new information and correct some errors. Thus here is the updated version.*

ANOTHER wave of glacial water slapped Reuben Burns directly in the ear and broke solidly over his head. A second or two later the wave was spent and Burns felt himself sliding down the backside of the swell. When his ears cleared, he could once again hear the wind roaring past. It was the first hours of Friday, September 10th, 1875, and Lake Michigan wanted to swallow him whole, of that he was sure. With his elbows and knees he tried to get a better grip on the piece of wreckage that was now his life raft. Again he felt himself quickly raised up the side of another wave. Tucking his chin to his chest, he held his breath as the whitecap slapped him once more. His hands were too numb for him to know if he still had a good grip on the shattered pilothouse that was keeping him afloat. It seemed as if the waves would never stop coming until finally one overwhelmed him. The night was so dark that he could not distinguish the sky from the seas. His sole companion in this suffering was the boat's second cook, adrift and semi-conscious on the same wreckage. It probably would have been of little comfort had Burns known they were far from alone in this plight, for nearby were the drifting survivors of another shattered laker and soon there would be the crew of a third boat.

As the bright orange sun pushed over the horizon it brought no hint of warmth, only light; light that revealed the second cook's lifeless form as it slipped from the makeshift raft and vanished into what remained of the waves. Burns knew that before long it would be his body drifting away. Overhead the sky had turned bright blue with puffy cold clouds rushing past. The wind still whistled with a vengeance and the lake was a green-gray color that occasionally reflected the blue sky. Summoning the strength to lift his head, Burns looked around the cantankerous horizon. Perhaps it was better that he did not know that he was floating, powerless, right in the middle of Lake Michigan, over 20 miles from land.

Through the bitter day Reuben Burns drifted atop his wreckage raft. As he saw the sun sinking toward the west, he felt his strength sinking as well. Also coming soon would be the coming of the dark night and the air would get colder. He knew all too well that in the night the lake would digest him and leave not a trace. Like an open-handed insult it continued to slap him, one wave after another. Through the day several schooners had passed in the distance, each one draining a little of his hope with it. There was no reason to believe that the coming night would be any different.

Downbound for Chicago, plowing through Lake Michigan's chop came the schooner *Havana*. The 306-ton, 135-foot schooner had the wind at her heels and was making good time down the lake. Shortly before seven o'clock in the evening, those aboard the *Havana* spotted something bobbing in the waves, large and white and from a distance no regular shape. Striking her sails, Captain Hugh Ross had the schooner slowed and drew near the object. Floating ahead was what seemed to be the remains of a steamer's pilothouse and clinging to it there appeared to be the body of a dead crewman. With pike-poles at the ready, the schooner's crew prepared to recover the floater, but as they drew close, the body suddenly stirred and came to life with a feeble wave. In short order the refugee was pulled over the rail, but the lake had left him semiconscious, so the *Havana's* crew quickly carried him to the shelter of the schooner's fo'c'sle. It would be awhile before he could mutter more than his name and that of his vessel, the *Equinox*.

Like many similar boats of her era, the Equinox *and her near-twin* Mendota *sailed the lakes, carrying passengers and anything that would fit in her hold.*

ALL HANDS ON DECK

Unknown to those aboard the *Havana*, there was another schooner that held a different piece of the *Equinox's* puzzle. The wind-grabber *Emma A. Mayes* was met by the tug *Protection* off Chicago and brought into the harbor. As the schooner nudged up to the pier, her master Captain Edward Lusk wasted no time in telling the story of the *Mayes* and her towing steamer *Equinox*. The *Mayes* herself was in rough shape. Heeled over in a bad list, with her cargo shifted, the schooner was sporting a badly split foresail. It was evident that only through the skill of her crew had the sailing vessel managed to come safely off the lake.

A week before the *Emma A. Mayes* turned up in Chicago, the story of the *Equinox* started far up the twisting murk of the Saginaw River at an East Saginaw dock. There the slow process of loading a cargo of 5,130 barrels of salt consigned to Chicago was proceeding. Constructed in 1857 at Buffalo, New York, by Frederick Nelson Jones, the *Equinox* was a typical Great Lakes propeller of the day. Sliding off the builder's ways at the Ohio Street shipyard between Chicago and Wabash streets, her sleek wooden hull had all of the characteristics of a true monster. From her stern rail along her graceful curving deck to the peak of her high bluff bow she measured 187-feet long, 620 tons burden, with a steam power plant that could produce 448 horsepower. Across her deck she spanned 31 feet between her tall hogging arches. Passenger accommodations were affixed to the main deck and atop it a multi-sided pilothouse. Below these fixtures was an enclosed cargo deck that was accessible through side-port gangways. She could carry almost any cargo below decks, from barreled flour to teams of horses. The whole profile was crowned aft with a tall smoke-stack and forward with a single towering mast.

Enrolled into service at the Buffalo Creek District on May 12th, 1857, the propeller *Equinox* was owned by the

Dean Richmond concerns. In 1865, these same operators had a tween-decks added to her hold, probably to better facilitate the carrying of barreled cargo. As of September 13th, 1865, her new tonnage was 870.51, consistent with such a modification. Dean Richmond sold the *Equinox* in May of 1867. That year she began running for the Union Steamboat Company between Buffalo and Chicago. This was a route that would become the regular path for most of the boat's career.

By that summer-like Sunday along the Saginaw waterfront in 1875, the *Equinox* was owned by the Cleveland partnership Garrison and Scott, the latter being the boat's Master, Captain Dwight Scott. In the background of the vessel's management were two silent partners, W.H. Sullivan and Captain John Pridgeon, both of Detroit. Captain Pridgeon was one of the most prominent vessel barons around the Great Lakes and managed to hold interest in a large fleet of lakeboats. Many of his lakers ran between Sarnia, Ontario and Chicago. So dominating was his influence along this passage that in marine circles the route had been dubbed "Pridgeon's Line" implying that the stretch of water up Lake Huron, through the Straits of Mackinac and down to Chicago was owned by the captain and his fleet.

The *Equinox* had spent her fair share running along Pridgeon's Line, but the most recent contract had brought her to Saginaw. In 18 seasons of service the big wooden steamer had worked hard and the stresses of her toil were beginning to show. One fact that demonstrated this was that the insurance rating of the once elegant steamer had slipped to B1. This was not surprising, considering her advancing age. In tow of the *Equinox* this trip would be the schooner *Emma A. Mayes*, Captain Lusk's command. This would be only the second trip for the *Equinox* with the *Mayes* as consort. For an extended period of time the steamer had been paired with the 139-foot schooner *Guiding Star*, but the officers of the two boats had apparently had some kind of falling out and the partnering of the two had been terminated. Surely what consort was attached to her stern mattered little to the *Equinox*, for she seemed more than prepared to hiss her way once more along Pridgeon's Line.

Supervising the loading of Captain Scott's *Equinox* as she took the last barrels of salt was First Mate Cyrus Woodruff, who was a captain in his own right. Formerly the master of the *Milton D. Ward*, Mate Woodruff had been caught up in the ebb and flow of Great Lakes commerce and found himself earning his living as the number two man aboard the *Equinox*. Even in modern times it is not unusual for a certified master of vessels to work on occasion as mate. In fact, this practice has become almost a tradition on the lakes.

Also aboard the *Equinox* were two special passengers on a late season sabbatical. From the shelter of the Sacred Heart convent in Detroit, Captain Scott's 19-year-old daughter Minnie had come to visit her father and to experience the adventure of the wild lakes. Accompanying her was the captain's 17-year-old granddaughter, Hattie. For Captain Scott, whose spouse had passed away several years before, the company of the two maidens was an incredible treat. The business of the *Equinox* kept him away from these apples of his eye for nearly eight months of each year yet they were his only family. When a person is away like that time passes swiftly, friends who are seen just during the winter months and relatives who are spoken to only at holidays appear to age unexpectedly. Likewise, children grow up at a breathtaking rate, seeming almost to be a different person each time they are encountered. Naturally Captain Scott was delighted to have the young ladies aboard and made sure they were shown all of the boat's best courtesy. Obviously the atmosphere about the *Equinox* was light-hearted and relaxed. This was also an era when some of the non-licensed crew were simple drifters with a taste for demon rum and captains were virtual tyrants, so when the old man is happy, the crew is cheerful.

There is an old superstition that says nothing good can come from a voyage that is started on a Sunday. Of course every time something goes afoul with some luckless laker, those who subscribe to such legend search for her day of departure to fulfill the fable. With no regard for the Sunday fallacy, the jovial *Equinox* steamed from the Saginaw dock with the schooner *Emma A. Mayes* dutifully in tow astern on Sunday, September 5th, 1875. Early Monday found the two boats creeping up the widening expanse of Saginaw Bay. The weather Lake Huron was presenting was a breath of summer belated, and up in the *Equinox's* pilothouse, Mate Woodruff had the majority of the boat's windows lowered, allowing the freshwater breeze to drift through. Flanking the mate and enjoying the fine day was the boat's wheelsman Reuben Burns. Surely the feeling was that this was the way to start a trip to Chicago!

All around the *Equinox*, cabin windows and doors were propped open and those not hard at work with the daily chores found good reason to go out on deck. Along the cargo deck the top half of a number of the gangways was opened to the breeze and strung up at the boat's promenade was a small load of laundry that waved toward the *Emma A. Mayes*.

From the schooner, Captain Lusk kept a casual eye on the steamer as it churned ahead in the sticky haze. If it were not for the lake's cool breath, the day might even have been considered uncomfortable. As darkness closed in Monday evening, the *Equinox* and consort were coming abeam

Sturgeon Point, their lights illuminating the cabin windows as a row of amber squares. From shore, that was the image that marked the passing lakers, a simple row of amber lights floating like a ghost across the lake's distance. Everyone aboard the two boats held out the hope that the current weather conditions would prevail all along the 500 odd miles of Pridgeon's Line that stretched to Chicago.

By Tuesday afternoon it appeared that summer was about to expire. To the west the sky had become unfriendly and dark gray, swallowing the sun long before it hit the horizon. From the rail of the *Mayes*, Captain Lusk gazed toward the blackening distance. His instincts told him that the dark curtain to the west predictably marked the last act of the summer's fair weather festival. Since there was no form of weather reporting or forecasting available to the *Equinox* and *Mayes*, no one aboard the boats had any way of knowing that the line of dark clouds marked the leading squall of a powerful and fast-moving cold front trailing more than 250 miles to the west. Behind the front, a strong northeast flow of air built gale-force winds and the whole nightmare was headed directly for Lake Michigan.

By 4 p.m., a sinister quiet had fallen upon the pair of lakers. From the *Emma A. Mayes* it was easy to hear the voices of those on the *Equinox*, as well as the clanks and hisses of the work aboard her, echoing across the water. The sky now appeared divided in half and Captain Lusk could clearly see the flashes of lightning followed by long-delayed thunder. In anticipation of the coming weather, the schooner's master had put the crew to work securing the boat for rough weather. As they worked, the time span between flashes of lightning and the thunder shortened as the storm was charging closer. This merely added to the urgency of the crew's work as they attempted to ready the boat. Swiftly the winds began to freshen and moments later the rain came in whipping sheets. The precipitation strafed horizontally ahead of the shrieking wind and the seas came up instantly, having built over the 50-plus miles between the Wisconsin shore and the two boats. The waves quickly set the pair of lakers on their beams ends with a continual rolling action. Surely, this was a powerful system, out to test every vessel in its path.

Unknown to those aboard the *Equinox* and *Mayes*, another team of lakers was being set upon by the squall just a few scant miles behind. When approaching Mackinaw, the steamer *Mendota* and her two-barge tow found themselves assaulted by the southwest storm. To say that the *Equinox* and *Mendota* were two of a kind would not be correct, but to say that they were of the same class of vessel would be much closer. Constructed at Cleveland just three months after the *Equinox* entered service, the *Mendota* was of 785 tons burden and basically outfitted the same. Equipped with side ports to her cargo deck as well as passenger accommodations on top, the steamer was of screw propulsion and able to pull a string of loaded schooners. Upon her enrollment the *Mendota* went straight to work for up-start vesselman William Crosthwaite.

In command of the *Mendota* on this rough 1875 autumn passage was Captain A.S. Fairbanks and behind the steamer were the schooner-barges *Morning Star* and *Evening Star*, all being bound for Chicago along Pridgeon's Line. Onboard for this trip was a special guest, William S. Crosthwaite Jr., the 21-year-old son of the *Mendota's* owner. Unlike the guests aboard the *Equinox*, young Crosthwaite was a bit reluctant to be aboard the *Mendota*. He felt deep down that somehow the family maritime business was not his true calling. Unfortunately, the pressures for a son to follow in his father's footsteps were far greater in the starched collar days of the 1870s than they are today, so William Jr. found himself aboard the *Mendota*, reluctantly, to learn the business.

ALL HANDS ON DECK

At midnight on the first day of September, the *Mendota* departed Buffalo with her schooner-barges. All three had full loads of coal aboard as they enjoyed fair weather crossing Lake Erie. Although their progress was slow, the three vessels made the St. Clair River and by midnight Saturday they tied up at Stanley's Dock. There the boat took on 89 cords of wood to fuel their passage to Chicago. Just like the *Equinox*, the *Mendota* departed on her leg to Chicago on Sunday morning.

Although the *Mendota* and her consorts were slow, their passage up the thumb of Michigan and into the width of Lake Huron actually went faster than the *Equinox's* passage up the twisting Saginaw River. At their snail's pace it took the *Mendota* and her consorts a full three days to get to the Straits of Mackinac. The weather had remained fair all the way up, but as the little fleet passed the McGulpin Point light, the wind began to freshen and the squall approached.

Shortly before the squall struck the *Mendota* and her consorts, Captain Fairbanks decided that he did not like the dusting that his boat was being exposed to and elected to run for shelter. Turning just a couple of points to the south, he ducked the trio behind a point which would afford lee from a southwest wind. Before the boats reached that shelter, the squall passed and the winds died from a shriek to a bluster. With winds continuing from the southwest, Captain Fairbanks elected to shelter after passing the Manitou Islands, knowing that such a wind would build waves the full length of Lake Michigan. In such a sea the captain did not want to find himself, so the *Mendota* would push into Glen Arbor and reportedly lay at the "Kelderhouse dock" until the lake simmered down. Once in shelter the steamer rafted to her two schooner-barges and simply waited. Meanwhile, out on the open lake, the *Equinox* and her consort sailed past on their way toward disaster.

ALONG PRIDGEON'S LINE

At two o'clock Thursday afternoon, the *Mendota* and her barges set out once again down Lake Michigan. Shortly after the three boats had rolled onto the open lake, the winds began to shift rapidly to the northwest and blow a gale. All the boats were taking quite a beating from the following sea that had developed ahead of the winds, so again Captain Fairbanks turned the *Mendota*. This time his maneuver was an effort to run against the seas toward the shelter of South Manitou Island. After pounding head to the wind for some time, Captain Fairbanks determined that the trio was making no headway and turned yet another time to flee before the wind.

Both the *Mendota* and *Equinox* were headed toward Chicago with a full gale at their heels with the *Equinox* now being nearly four hours in the lead. Both boats were almost two full days tardy in moving down the lake. While a written record of the movements of Captain Fairbanks' boat exists, there are none from Captain Scott's *Equinox*. Considering that the two boats were delayed by nearly the exact same interval, it is safe to reason that Captain Scott's actions in avoiding the storm were similar to those of Captain Fairbanks with the *Mendota*. It mattered little, as now both boats were deeply into Lake Michigan's grip.

On the schooner *Emma A. Mayes*, Captain Lusk, like his counterpart Captain Scott aboard the towing steamer *Equinox*, had prepared for a storm, but expected nothing close to what Lake Michigan was delivering. The ripping wind instantly found the schooner's stowed canvas and began to unwrap it from her booms. Rolling to her gunwales, the *Mayes* was shipping water and in danger of being overwhelmed. All hands of the storm-tossed schooner took to the deck and rigging in an attempt to save their boat. As the crew of the *Mayes* struggled with her rigging, sudden shouts from the *Equinox* drew their attention. Bounding his way to the rolling schooner's bow, Captain Lusk tried to distinguish what was being shouted from the steamer. He thought he recognized the voice as that of Mate Woodruff and over the roaring of the wind it sounded as if he was calling "cast off your line, cast off your line," but it was difficult to understand.

It was clear that there was something radically wrong with the steamer *Equinox*, but the captain of the *Mayes* had his hands full saving his own boat. He had only time enough to release the tow line and then tend to the well-being of the schooner. As the line was let go, the screams of a female voice split the storm. "We're drowning! We're drowning!" the cries seemed to say. And with that, those aboard the *Mayes* watched in horror as the big steamer dipped, rolled onto her stern quarter and with a roar was swallowed by the lake leaving nothing but a hole in the water. Left peering through the darkness, the crew of the *Mayes* was in complete shock. The idea that a 187-foot lakeboat could plunge to the bottom in a matter of seconds was utterly unimaginable, but the fact remained there was only the lake where the *Equinox* had been moments before.

Alone in the storm, the crew of the *Mayes* now had to collect their wits and began to run with the winds. It was two o'clock Friday morning as they transitioned from witnesses to mariners once again. With what sails could be mustered, the schooner began pounding toward Chicago. There was no chance of searching for survivors in the pitch black night. The winds had now turned and were blowing out of the north, northeast, the waves had become mountainous and the temperature was beginning to plummet as Captain Lusk nursed his charge down the lake. Unknowingly he was leaving wheelsman Burns and the luckless second cook adrift on the *Equinox's* broken pilothouse.

ALONG PRIDGEON'S LINE

Nearly in the wake of the sunken *Equinox* came the *Mendota* and her barges, without an inkling of the disaster that had just occurred ahead. Captain Fairbanks, in fact, had the survival of his own boat foremost on his mind. It was back at a little past 10 o'clock that evening that First Mate John Coney was awakened by young William Crosthwaite Jr. He was told that the captain had ordered that Coney was to awaken all hands and get them to work rigging the pumps. Coney, a British immigrant, was a 20 year veteran of the mariner's profession with great experience both on the salt water seas and on the lakes. The word was that the *Mendota* had sprung a leak. When he got out on deck, Coney found that huge seas were boarding the vessel's stern and tons of water were cascading in wherever there was an opportunity. He immediately set his crew to work at the pumps. Three hand pumps as well as the steam siphon and bilge pump were put to work and for the next two hours they fought a desperate and losing battle against Lake Michigan. Coney made sure that every hatchway and opening was sealed as tightly as they could be, but it was no use, this was a losing battle with Lake Michigan.

About two o'clock came a lurch that was felt on the steamer as the towing hawser holding the *Morning Star* to the *Evening Star* parted leaving the *Morning Star* adrift in the maelstrom. An hour later the *Evening Star*, which had been first in the tow, was cut loose by the *Mendota's* crew under orders from Coney. This complicated matters for Captain James Bennett of the *Evening Star*, as his boat was already in a leaking condition and he needed all hands at the two pumps. The pumping operation would have to be halted, but only long enough so that the crew could man the sails. Meanwhile, from the *Mendota*, the lights of the two schooners seemed to simply vanish in the darkness.

Through the remainder of the night the *Mendota's* crew did all that they could to save their boat. Every hand not at the pumps was ordered to start dumping cordwood overboard in an effort to lighten the sinking steamer. As dawn began to brighten, one of the *Mendota's* huge arches fractured. These were the backbone of the boat and the point from where all of her load bearing strength was centered. It was a sure sign that she was breaking up. It was also something that sent a terrible cold fear toward every member of her crew. It was the complete realization that Lake Michigan was infinitely more powerful than their huge wooden lakeboat.

Next, the vessel's other arch was snapped like kindling and with that her engine and steam works began to rise up from below and shove through her wooden decks as the boat hogged in the seas. With that her steam pipes fractured and she rapidly hemorrhaged steam until all of her pressure was gone. Due to the loss of steam, her main pump quit working and then her forward pump became useless. It was all over for the *Mendota*.

At dawn Friday morning, both barges briefly became visible again from the *Mendota*. They appeared to have sails up and be making good weather of it, but the steamer was in a far different condition. Her fires out and the water nearly up to her deck, it was just a matter of time before she would go. An emergency sail had been raised, but after her steam went down it was promptly blown to rags by the wind. When all hope was given up, the crew was ordered to put on life vests and prepare the lifeboats. Captain Fairbanks' wife and father, who had been aboard for a pleasure trip, were each given two life belts, as if to insure their security. The captain, first mate, first engineer, two wheelsmen, two deck hands and William Crosthwaite launched one of the steamer's two lifeboats and were preparing to get away, when Crosthwaite spotted Mrs.

ALONG PRIDGEON'S LINE

Down to her rails, the Mendota *sinks while her barges fend for themselves. Author's Concept*

Fairbanks and the captain's father huddled near the pilothouse. Apparently, in the confusion, Captain Fairbanks had thought them to be in the other lifeboat. As the crowded yawl was lowering into the rolling seas, Crosthwaite leaped back onto the *Mendota's* cabin and struggled to the rescue of the two guests. When he reached the Fairbanks, the ship's cook was there as well, and the whole bunch began to struggle toward the yawl, which Captain Fairbanks was maneuvering back toward them. At that instant the *Mendota* sank like a stone beneath them shattering the deck houses and pulling the lifeboats and all aboard into a giant swirling vortex.

When William S. Crosthwaite surfaced, he was surrounded by heaving wreckage and struggling survivors. The yawl had been overturned and was carried off by the wind, so those lucky enough to surface alive began to cling to whatever pieces of the *Mendota* would keep them afloat. Crosthwaite, along with second engineer Ed Hughes, managed to crawl aboard a large chunk of the boat's crushed cabin and dragged the semi-conscious cook with them. In the distance they could see some of the *Mendota's* other people struggling to gather makeshift rafts. Now there were two groups of castaways drifting upon the remains of two different lakeboats within a few scant miles of one another. But Lake Michigan was not yet satisfied and set her ire toward yet another boat and crew.

With her sails finally set, the schooner-barge *Evening Star* had her crew hard at work on the pumps. By 11 o'clock Friday morning, Captain Bennett saw clearly that their efforts were useless. Some seven feet of lake water was filling her hold and she no longer answered to the helm. It was time to surrender the *Evening Star* to the lake and hope that the sacrifice would be enough to persuade the lake to spare the souls aboard. The order given, all seven of the schooner's crew jammed into the 15-foot yawl and abandoned the *Evening Star*. As the water sloshed aboard, the crew bailed for their lives and drifted before the storm. There were now three sets of castaways on the surface of Lake Michigan.

By daylight Friday, the *Equinox's* surviving consort *Emma A. Mayes* was in sight of land and by eight o'clock that same morning dropped her hooks just outside the port of Chicago. As a matter of routine, the tug *Protection* observed the schooner rocking at anchor and made a bee line out to claim her rightful towing charter. Safely in port, Captain Lusk and those of his crew spent the day telling of the tragic loss of the *Equinox*. Through that nasty Saturday the telegraphs clicked with reports of chaos across the lakes and by evening the compilation gave insight to the rude storm. The listings were incomplete as there was no mention of the *Mendota* or her barges.

ALONG PRIDGEON'S LINE

Having spent 27 hours adrift and constantly bailing, the crew of the *Evening Star* finally felt the stones and sand of the beach grind beneath the yawl boat. It was just after two o'clock Saturday afternoon when they dragged the boat clear of the lake near the town of Amsterdam and began to pace around and rub their limbs in an effort to cure the numbness. Captain Bennett had lost his boat, but apparently that was enough to satisfy the lake, at least in his case.

On Monday, two full days after the *Equinox* went to the bottom, the schooner *Havana* was towed into Chicago harbor. Onboard was Wheelsman Reuben Burns, now fully recovered from his odyssey on the shattered pilothouse. Shortly after the *Havana's* arrival, word spread along the waterfront that there was a survivor of the *Equinox* when all aboard were thought to have been lost. In quest of answers to the steamer's disaster, the curious as well as the professionals headed for the waterfront. Chief among them was Captain Lusk and the crew of the *Emma A. Mayes*. A crowd gathered at the *Havana* as Reuben Burns, flanked by Captain Ross, told his story. Those gathered around stood with wide eyes and intent ears as the sole survivor recalled the *Equinox's* last moments. Shortly after the storm hit the steamer and her consort, the *Equinox* began to roll heavily in the seas. Reuben Burns was at his post in the pilothouse with Captain Scott when the storm peaked and no sooner had the *Equinox* settled into her normal heavy weather posture, than the steamer sprung a leak on the port side aft. The leak was of massive proportions and it was all too clear that the *Equinox* was being overwhelmed. Captain Scott sent the mate aft to call to the *Mayes* and try to get her to "come along side," a shout that in the storm could easily be garbled to "cast off your line." Crowding on the fantail were most of the passengers and crew, but some of the crew took after the port lifeboat. That side of the boat was down the lowest and eleven men entered the boat and started lowering. Sensing that the boat was beginning to slip, Burns and Captain Scott abandoned the pilothouse and dashed aft toward the starboard lifeboat. Their scramble was far too late, for the *Equinox* heeled over on top of the port lifeboat and its occupants. The steamer sank beneath the running feet of the captain and wheelsman, with the captain catching the gangway and being pulled down. Burns and the second cook were lucky enough to pop up near the wreckage of the pilothouse and Burns was lucky enough to be seen by the *Havana*.

Late on Monday, the bark *Addie* sailed into Manitowoc, Wisconsin, and aboard were ten survivors with a story of their own. Greeting dry land across the sailing vessel's gangplank, came what remained of the *Mendota's* people, First Mate J. Coney, First Engineer Amos Ness, Franklin W. Fairbanks, Amos Wess, Scott Crone, A.S. Murphy, James Smith, L. Sage and George McKinney. Last of all came a heartbroken Captain Fairbanks who had lost his wife, father and his command to the lake in one bitter stroke. If an emptied soul existed anywhere on the lakes that day, it was his. All of the castaways were picked up Sunday evening when the *Addie* had stumbled onto the flotsam of the poor *Mendota*. What few persons the lake had spared were all now on dry land; the others, it was thought, would remain forever on Lake Michigan.

Originally, William Crosthwaite Jr., along with second engineer Ed Hughes, were reported as lost with the *Mendota*. Three days after the first load of survivors had been dropped off on dry land, the bark *Naiad* reported into the port of Chicago. Aboard her were the two missing men from the *Mendota*, William Crosthwaite Jr. and Ed Hughes.

In the weeks that followed the storm, there were investigations and summonses filed by the steamboat inspectors John P. Farrer and John B. Warren of the district of Chicago. All of this was overshadowed by the mystery that was evolving over the whereabouts of Reuben Burns, who although quite willing to talk about the *Equinox's* wreck when he came off the rescue schooner, had now vanished. There was great speculation that he had been spirited into hiding, or he was looking to sell his information to the inspectors, or to bleed the insurance companies who had underwritten the *Equinox*. In later days there appeared the following article in the *Chicago Inter Ocean*: "Private and special dispatches from Port Huron say a man has shipped on the propeller *St. Joseph*, who gives his name as Burns or Barr, and who claims to be the sole survivor of the propeller *Equinox*, but wants it kept quiet. No publicity will be given to the fact, as a matter of course, because that's what newspapers are for. Steamboat inspectors please take notice."

That simple paragraph, like the other news tid-bits concerning Burns, was meant to stir up as much mystery as possible in order to increase circulation. The fact was that the news reporting of the day was nearly as twisted as it is in modern times. Wheelsman Burns had his name mis-reported as Barr and Burr. There were even dramatic accounts of the sinkings, that had young Crosthwaite leaping aboard a sinking vessel to save his panicked wife and the two of them drowning in each other's arms. Crosthwaite was not married and the whole news item had been concocted. Yet it was picked up and printed by the Associated Press as fact. Additionally, the vessel that picked up the *Mendota's* lifeboat was, in one account, identified as being the schooner "*Idaho*." Over time, Burns got his wish and, like the *Equinox*, *Mendota*, *Evening Star* and *Morning Star*, faded into obscurity.

Young William S. Crosthwaite, in years to follow, found his true calling as a minister. What 1870s family could argue with such a calling? Surely the senior Mr. Crosthwaite could not. William Jr.'s calling took him to the wild west, across the Great Plains and into the American desert. Perhaps he felt a real need for a man of his calling in the west or perhaps the horror of Lake Michigan's frigid temper compelled him to travel as far from the water and the freshwater seas as he could get.

In all, the *Equinox* took 25 people to the bottom with her and the *Mendota* took 12 just four hours later, in virtually the same spot. More than a century ago and as of this writing they rest there, about eight miles off the Sable Points. It is a part of Lake Michigan where the bottom dips as low as several hundred feet and in places rises to less than 80-feet in depth. Literally hundreds of wrecks are scattered over this region and among them, undiscovered, are the *Equinox* and *Mendota*. Since 1875, they have been the obscure and unmarked grave of more than three dozen souls. On fair summer days, research divers in small boats armed with sidescan sonar, trace the bottom in quest of long-forgotten lakeboats. Year after year they act out this lonely, cold, damp obsession in the hope of casting a ray of light on the lost commands, homes and lives of the ones who made their careers on the lakes so long ago. Possibly this summer as these electronic explorers crisscross Lake Michigan, the pen will graph the image of a small wooden hulk and at last mark the grave of the *Equinox* or the *Mendota*. They are the sole monuments remaining of the people and vessels that once worked along Pridgeon's Line.

THE BEST LAID PLANS OF CHARLES EVANS

AS the wind whistled past his ears and the water in the bottom of his small boat sloshed around his benumbed feet, Charles Evans sat in the dark of night and waited for Lake Huron to impose her sentence upon him. The date was November 25th, 1870, and the charges being prosecuted against Evans consisted of theft, stupidity, incompetence and, worst of all, arrogance against the lake. As he shivered and prayed for forgiveness with his rear end frozen to the bench seat of his boat, he gave consideration to the crimes he had committed and the fact that his life was now subject to the whims of his judge and jury - the lake. The sentence for crimes such as those committed by Charles Evans, especially in November, was normally death.

Opportunity is the root of most crimes, and the circumstances that led Charles Evans into his misdeeds began in Chicago during the closing weeks of November when the schooner-barge *Montpelier* departed that port city in tow of the tug *George Brockway*. In the belly of the *Montpelier* was 20,233 bushels of corn bound for Ogdensburg, New York. Pleasant breezes of Indian summer had been hovering over the southern Great Lakes as the *Montpelier* departed Chicago, but as the two boats pushed into lower Lake Huron on Tuesday evening, November 22nd, the weather conditions took an about-face. The winds came out of the west, screaming like November should. Along with the frozen breath of the November witch, came her curtain of blinding snow that swept along a stage of sharp, white-bearded waves. The *Montpelier's* hull was fairly new, having first slid into the freshwater seas just four seasons earlier, and she was doing well against the waves. Her hull timbers were holding their place and she was hardly leaking more than a tea cup of water in any one place. She appeared to be water tight enough to easily roll her way into Port Huron. The problem, however, would be with her tug.

Although being a year younger than the *Montpelier*, the 112-foot long tug *Brockway* was having more than a little difficulty handling the 138-foot schooner-barge in the storm. The tugs of her era had a cabin arrangement that made it difficult, and at times impossible for her crew to venture out on deck in heavy weather to handle the towlines. These tugs were constructed favoring ease of construction rather than ease of handling and their cabin arrangement was such that a crew member was likely to be washed overboard if they ventured outside in high seas. To make matters worse, the tug and her consort were running nearly blind in the snowstorm. So, when the Canadian shore reached out and bit the two vessels, it was somewhat expected.

Although both boats were hard aground, the shores on this side of the lake have always been sandy. Had the vessels been run ashore on the opposite side of Lake Huron, they would have been rapidly chewed to pieces by the boulders and rocks. Thus the waves bursting over the two hulls may have looked spectacular, but they were far from fatal. By the following day, the gale had faded and the seas had gone down leaving both the *Brockway* and the *Montpelier* close to being high and dry. The crews made shore safely and worked their way to Sarnia. As it turned out, the boats had run ashore just four miles from Point Edward and in short order the wrecking vessel *Rescue* was on the scene. The

THE BEST LAID PLANS OF CHARLES EVANS

Brockway was easily pulled from its stranded position, but the fully loaded *Montpelier* would require lightering and favorable weather conditions. In general the conclusion was that she would have to sit for a while, in fact, she may have to sit there until spring.

Word quickly spread that a big schooner, fully loaded with Chicago corn, was fetched up on the beach. The stories, of course, grew to say that she may be a total loss and keen ears soon picked up on the implications. Indeed, to some people, the thought of a ship load of corn just laying there, was more like treasure waiting for the taking. One such person was a farmer by the name of Charles Evans who lived just two miles down the shore from the *Montpelier's* resting place.

On the afternoon before his crime, Evans gathered up his tools for stealing. A small rowboat and 20 empty sacks were all that he thought he would need to make a quick trip up to the wreck and then return with enough corn to feed his livestock for a few months. He had fashioned a small sail to help him along his way and supplemented it with rowing oars. As he loaded up and prepared to leave, however, he found that one of his oars was badly cracked. A quick repair with some lash cloth was made to the propulsion device as Evans waited for darkness to set in.

It was a perfect night for any thief - the darkness nearly swallowed the boat as Charles Evans silently sailed his way from the beach and headed up toward the *Montpelier*. A steady breeze from the southwest aided him along in his trip. Gentle swells rolled beneath his little boat and he could clearly see the lights at the mouth of the Saint Clair River. Judging by the location of those same lights he set his course toward the wreck. The two mile trip was easy and soon he was at the hulk of the *Montpelier*. She lay there heeled over on her beam ends, her hull fully intact. It must have been clear to Evans that some earlier thieves had already "visited" the *Montpelier* prior to his arrival. He found her hatches wide open and went straight to work filling his big sacks with golden corn. Working as fast as any thief, Evans filled one bag at a time and then went down to the lower rail and parked the bags there. He was feeling a sense of thieves' glee at getting a lot of something for nothing - what a steal.

Throughout most of civilization, there usually has been a system by which any given society deals with a thief. In western civilization there is the law enforcement officer and the judge and, if needed, the jury. On the Great Lakes, the lake itself serves all three of these positions. Even as Charles Evans, the now self-proclaimed master thief of corn, was working at filling the last of his 20 bags - Lake Huron was about to serve him up some karmic justice of its own. Almost unnoticed by the busy thief of corn, that southwest breeze that had helped him on his way to the *Montpelier* had now shifted to blowing out of due south. To make matters worse, the wind had also strengthened. Being on the leeward side of the heeled over wreck, Evans could not feel the newly formed choppy waves that were slapping at the wreck. Even if he could have heard or felt the change in conditions, it is likely that Evans was now too focused on his stolen corn to care.

With the last of his 20 sacks fully stuffed with stolen corn, Evans paused for a moment of satisfaction as he gazed upon his ill-gotten gain. Then he began the effort of moving the bags into his tiny boat. It was then that the realization hit him that there was simply no way to fit all of those bags, plus himself, into that little boat! He decided to simply take as many as he could. The task must have been much more difficult than Evans had expected. The little boat threatened to capsize each time he moved a bag aboard and the lake took every opportunity to lap over the rail and slosh around

THE BEST LAID PLANS OF CHARLES EVANS

at his feet in a stinging pool of ice water. The night's air had grown bitter cold and before long his hands were numb and hardly able to handle the sacks. By the time that Evans had about 15 of the 20 bags aboard his midget getaway boat, he decided he had enough and struggled to get away from the wrecked *Montpelier*.

Being about as overloaded as it could get without simply sinking, the little rowboat was moved along the *Montpelier's* hull by Evans, hand over hand. Only after swinging around the wreck's end did he suddenly feel the hand of Lake Huron's justice. Almost immediately the waves threatened to swamp the boat and Evans scrambled to set his oars. On the first stroke the repair job that he had cobbled on the broken oar failed and he was left with just the handle in his hand. The propulsive end of the oar simply vanished into the blackness as Evans watched helplessly. His next move was to set his makeshift sail. That plan rapidly went down the dumper as the winds on the sail were simply taking him out into the open lake. Thinking as fast as he was able, Evans worked to unseat the other oar in the hope of getting it into position to act as a rudder. In the darkness and with his fingers benumbed by the cold, he fumbled the oar and it too splashed into the lake and was swallowed by the water. Now Evans had no choice other than to take down his little sail and place himself at the mercy of a merciless Lake Huron.

Back at the farm, the Evans family had expected Charles home by morning. Saturday morning, afternoon, evening and night came and went and Charles did not return. With the weather growing more ugly as the day went by, Charles' next of kin grew ever more concerned that they may soon be officially titled his next of kin. As dawn broke on Sunday, they were all thinking that Lake Huron had taken him from them.

Charles Evans, in fact, was alive this entire time - although he was far from being "well." For a full 18 hours he sat in his little boat surrounded by those big sacks of corn. Through the entire day Saturday, the wind stung his skin and countless waves threatened to sink him. He waved at dozens of boats passing in the distance, yet no one saw him. As the night came once again, Evans was beginning to believe he may not see the next morning. The layers of warm clothing he was wearing were now soaked in all of the worst places and if his boat were to sink, he may as well have been wearing a suit of cement as they would weigh him down and take him straight to the bottom of the lake.

In the darkness, as Saturday turned into Sunday, Evans had more than enough time to contemplate his crime, his greed and most of all his stupidity. Were the 15 sacks of corn that he had stolen really worth his life? Regret and despair seemed to come naturally with the cold and darkness as he sat and waited for Lake Huron to deliver his fate. And deliver his fate, she did.

Little noticed by Evans, shortly after sunset Saturday the winds shifted once again. This time the winds swung around and began to blow out of the west, southwest. In the deep blackness of that night, he was likely unaware that the winds were now blowing him ever closer to the safety of the Canadian shore.

It is likely that the first hint that Charles Evans had that he may just survive after all, was the sound of the waves on the sandy beach. As the overloaded rowboat's keel skidded against the lake's bottom, Evans had Lake Huron's permission to leave the boat and go ashore. Cold, hungry and exhausted, he went looking for the nearest farm house. He had been blown 20 miles up the lake.

Times were a lot different in 1870 and when someone came beating on your door in the middle of the night, you

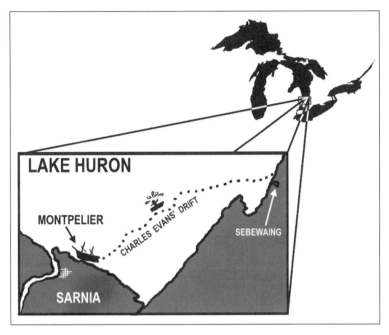

answered with compassion. Additionally, when you lived on the shore of the lakes, and it was the month of November, having a castaway from the lake coming to ask for help was somewhat expected. Evans was thawed out, fed and had his clothing dried by the fire. He confessed his misdeed to the farmer who offered to hitch up his team of horses and wagon and take Evans' boat down to Point Edward... in exchange for some of the corn. Evans, by this time, wanted nothing more to do with that corn and told the farmer he could have it all. Keeping his word, at dawn on Sunday the farmer hitched up his team and, with Evans, went down the beach and recovered his rowboat and all of the sacks of corn. Once the corn was safely stashed in his barn, the farmer took Charles Evans the 20 miles to Point Edward where the boat was parked and Evans departed to walk the rest of the way home feeling as if he was lucky to just be alive.

ALL HANDS ON DECK

Later in the week, the Coast Wrecking Company's steamer *Rescue* and her wrecking crew returned to the *Montpelier*. Their first task was to lighter the boat and required shoveling several tons of corn into the lake. The corn cargo that was thrown overboard was simply written off as a cost involved in saving the vessel itself. The *Montpelier* was then put on an even keel and with minimal pumping was hauled into deep water, returned to Port Huron and subsequently returned to service.

Although colorful would not describe the career of the *Montpelier*, the word "long" would apply. Before her grounding detailed in this story, she had already been shoved ashore at least once before in her four previous years of service. In the 1869 season she had lost her first recorded battle with Lake Huron and found herself fetched up at Presque Isle. Just five months after her grounding at Point Edward, in the first days of April, 1871, she collided with the schooner *Maggie Thompson* at Chicago. Then, as if to tempt Charles Evans once again, she once again went ashore with a grain cargo at Point Edward at the end of summer, 1871. It is a safe bet that Evans stayed far away from her on that occasion.

Perhaps the *Montpelier's* greatest escape came on the night of Friday, November 1st, 1878, when a destructive Lake Michigan gale tossed her and the schooners *America* and *Australian* ashore at Grand Haven, Michigan. Although all of the *Montpelier's* crew escaped, as did the entire crew of the *America*, the *Australian* lost a single crewman to the lake. From Chicago, the tug *Niagara* was dispatched with a steam pump and orders to free the *Montpelier*. Four days later, the *Niagara* sent a message back to Chicago that the *Montpelier* would not pump out. The boat was impaled on a couple of old wrecks north of the Grand Haven pier and the wrecks had

100

THE BEST LAID PLANS OF CHARLES EVANS

badly damaged the *Montpelier's* hull. At the time it was reported, perhaps embellished, that some 20 wrecks were located in a natural graveyard of old schooners in that same location. By November 10th, the *Montpelier* had been stripped of her anchors and any other fixtures, yet the following day wrecking master Captain Blackburn went to work on her with a larger steam pump. Six days later, Mr. W. F. Merrick, the vessel's responsible agent stated that the *Montpelier* was abandoned as a total wreck. This would have been the end if not for Mr. Hull a Muskegon opportunist who purchased the abandoned boat 10 days later for just $350. The following spring the wreck was chipped from the ice, pumped dry and towed to Kirby's shipyard where she was repaired and returned to service. *Montpelier* went back to work carrying her same name plus untold tons of grain cargo and board-feet of lumber. Mr. Hull, had indeed made a terrific deal when he bought the sad wreck of the *Montpelier*.

Montpelier continued to work for nearly three full decades. Her old timbers finally gave out on August 11, 1907 when she suffered a hull failure while tied up to a dock on the Detroit River. She sank and was written off for the second and final time as a total loss.

As of this writing, there are no records found as to how long Charles Evans was around, but he probably never stole any more shipwreck corn, or anything else.

CHRISTENED WITH WATER - INTERRED WITH DYNAMITE

GRAY clouds hung low over Port Huron while cold blusters of wind whipped frigid rain from the darkened sky, but this was not the foreboding of the loss of another lake vessel. Instead the unpleasant weather conditions were the window dressing for the birth of a new, huge, lakeboat. It was Saturday evening the 22nd day of April, 1871, and poised on the builder's ways at the Muir and Livingston shipyard was a schooner that measured larger than any other on the western lakes. Work on her had been going on for the past eight months and she was considered a true masterpiece of the shipbuilder's art. Now, in spite of the awful weather, hundreds of spectators had gathered on both sides of the Black River just to see her launched.

Spectacular was the best way to describe the wooden hull that the rains were soaking. It measured 210 feet in keel and 35 feet across its beam. Eight hatchways would allow for cargo loading and three tall masts would be used to hoist her sails. The hold where her cargo would be carried measured 19 feet 10 inches deep at its maximum point and 14 feet deep at its shallowest point. Her deck timbers were three inches thick and below that each of the huge wooden beams that supported the decking were wrought-iron hanging knees. Each hanging knee weighed 30 pounds and the sum cost for all of them was $2,500 - a whopping sum in 1871. Along the outside of her hull the timbers were strengthened by a webbing of wrought-iron straps bolted to her. Most unique in her design, however, were her "leeboards." Leeboards were huge, flat, rudder-like planks that were bolted to the vessel's sides by a single rod that acted as a pivot. When running in deep water, the boat would lower its leeboard and it would act like a centerboard and enhance stability. When the vessel entered shallow waters, the crew could use a simple block and tackle to retract the leeboard. In lakes history, only three sailing merchant vessels are known to have been equipped with leeboards. Overall, the new vessel was the most modern and well equipped schooner on the lakes and all of that came at a cost of $60,000.

Waiting to take command of the new vessel as soon as her keel touched the water was Captain Charles Elphicke. Standing next to the vessel's soon-to-be master was his wife and, in her hand was the bottle that would be broken over the bow in the christening. Traditionally, that bottle contains champagne, but for reasons that were never recorded, this occasion's bottle contained a mixture of water and molasses. By five o'clock that evening, the heavy wooden blocks that held the vessel on the launching ways had been hammered out and she rested on her own weight. She did not, however, slide down into the water. Considering the vessel's mass, the shipyard officials were well prepared for this contingency. Hydraulic jacks were at the ready and once muscled into place, they began working in harmony to break the inertia of the squatting vessel. At nearly six o'clock on the button, the big schooner slid into the Black River.

Also in consideration of the boat's mass, the shipyard officials had hired the tug *Burnside* to stand by the new boat's stern with a line aboard. This was a measure to ensure that when launched the big schooner would not just keep going and slam into the heavily populated opposite bank of the river. Unfortunately, as the big hull splashed sideways into the river, that safety line and tug were instantly mooted by the big schooner's mass. The tug went into full ahead on her engine, the line stiffened bar-tight and the huge schooner just kept going. Over on the opposite shore, Mr. Peache had been watching the launching from the rear of his boiler shop. No doubt he and his helpers had been watching for the past eight months as the vessel grew from a few timbers into an elegant schooner. There was no way that they were going to miss the launch. Now, as Mr. Peache cheered at the splash, his joy suddenly turned to terror as the stern of the massive schooner came directly toward both him and his shop. Dropping tools and stumbling over one another, the boiler makers scrambled for the front of the shop and any opening leading to the street as the timbers of the vessel crunched into the worn wood of the back of the shop. With a sickening noise, the new schooner bounced off the shop and drifted back into the open river. In short order the tug regained control over the schooner and parked it back at the shipyard's fit-out pier. Meanwhile, Mr. Peache and his staff had a lot better view of the shipyard from the hole in the wall of the back of the shop.

Once the new schooner was secured at the fit-out dock, Mrs. Elphicke made her way down to the bow and announced "I christen you the *James C. Couch*" as she smashed the bottle of water and molasses over the boat's bow. At that moment, a giant flag with the vessel's name on it was raised from her mast. Work began immediately at making the new vessel ready for service and no sooner had the work began than the vessel's critics began scoffing.

Many who were considered to be "experts" in the maritime community considered the general size of the *James C. Couch* to be more than a risk. Her cargo capacity of carrying a projected 1-million board-feet of lumber seemed impractical. Her leeboards seemed unworkable to many an old tar as well. But worst of all was the fact that she had been christened with water. Water christenings have always been considered to be bad luck and thus many mariners considered the *James C. Couch* to be doomed as soon as the bottle had been broken across her bow.

Most of the scoffs of the *Couch's* critics seemed to come true almost immediately. On her first trip with cargo aboard, the *Couch* carried 1-million board-feet of lumber out of the Saginaw River and ran into trouble on Lake Huron. Some heavy spring weather had blown up and the deck load was simply too much. Although she lost some of it, she managed to stagger to Charity Island and anchor. The steamer *East Saginaw* came out to the *Couch* and lightered her to the tune of 200,000 board-feet of lumber. With her deck load reduced the schooner pressed on to Chicago without additional trouble. The next prediction of the critics to come true involved her leeboards. They proved to be neither as effective, or as handy as her builders had hoped. Although there is no record of them being removed, there are accounts that she was headed to a Detroit shipyard to have them removed and have a common centerboard installed. Now the only prophecy remaining was that of the hoo-doo of having her christened with water. Many of the critics were sure that she was doomed.

When criticism is based on engineering or actual experience, it often comes true. When it is based on superstition, however, the results are as predictable as the science they are based on. Of course critics will wait a lifetime for their prophecy to self fulfill - in the case of the *Couch*, they would have a very long wait. In spite of the superstition, the *James C. Couch* went on to outlive many of her critics. Of course, she had her share of scrapes and dings, but largely she remained one of the most productive vessels on the Great Lakes.

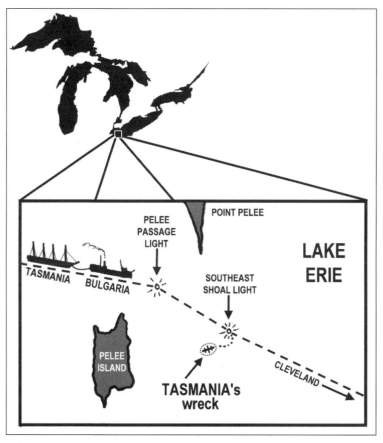

PELEE PASSAGE LIGHT

POINT PELEE

TASMANIA

BULGARIA

SOUTHEAST SHOAL LIGHT

LAKE ERIE

PELEE ISLAND

TASMANIA's wreck

CLEVELAND

In late August of 1882, the *Couch's* most famous oddity took place. The last Tuesday of that month found the *Couch* on her way down Lake Michigan. When she was about 30 miles north of Chicago, the tug *J.A. Crawford* headed out to pick her up and tow her into the harbor. No sooner had the tug gotten her hawser attached to the *Couch*, than the *Crawford's* captain found that the winds were pushing the schooner faster than the tug could run. With that being apparent, Captain Gorman of the *Crawford* called down and had the tug's engine stopped. The big schooner then towed the tug all the way to Chicago. The marine reporters of the day claimed that it was the first time that a schooner had towed a tug.

In 1890, the *Couch* changed ownership as she was purchased into the fleet of James Corrigan and re-named *Tasmania*. From then on she would carry long-haul iron ore from the upper lakes normally as consort to the steamer *Bulgaria*. Corrigan had purchased the *Bulgaria* three years earlier while she was still under construction at the West Bay City shipyard of wooden shipbuilding genius James Davidson. Now the giant wooden steamer would have a consort of equal ilk. Often paired together the two lakers did a fine job for Captain Corrigan's fleet for the next 15 years.

Autumn 1905 would turn out to be the most disastrous on the lakes since the beginning of the industrial revolution. For the first time in lakes history both the wooden and the steel giant lakeboats would be overcome by the fury of the autumn gales. Steaming directly into the middle of this horrible shipping season came the *Bulgaria* and *Tasmania*.

Bellies full of Escanaba iron ore were the burden of the *Bulgaria*, *Tasmania* and the third member of their party, the schooner-barge *Ashland*. With the *Tasmania* taking the rear position in the string of three vessels, they had made a good trip down Lake Huron and spent most of Thursday winding their way down the Saint Clair and Detroit rivers. As they came downbound, the weather began to fall apart in a classic late October pattern. Unknown to the mariners, this storm would be far stronger than most storms seen in October. Sometime after midnight the ore-laden trio exited the lower Detroit River with every intention of heading toward their destination of Cleveland.

On this black night the *Tasmania* was under the command of Captain William Radford assisted by First Mate George Whitesall, both being residents of Courtright, Ontario. Also serving on the schooner-barge were engineer Austin Mayhew, seamen Michael Boyle, August Ulbrick, John Trapp, J.R. Stough and Harry Lapask. As the *Tasmania* entered the darkness of the open lake it was immediately apparent that they had made a big mistake. One well-known characteristic of Lake Erie is that it is so shallow that any sort of storm quickly builds steep waves. Now the seas had come up and began pounding at all three vessels while they were still within sight of the Detroit River light. Although the steamer was able to haul over onto the course for Pelee Passage, it would have been very difficult for the *Bulgaria* to turn all the way around and pull the boats back to the safety of the river. Additionally, although the storm seemed to be growing stronger, there was really no need for drastic action. All three vessels had seen similar weather many times in the past and none of them seemed in distress at the moment. Their best bet was to head through the passage and press on to Cleveland.

We often read accounts of storms, such as the one that the *Tasmania* and the vessels she was tied to found themselves in that night. These accounts often use eyewitness descriptions of the waves with words such as "mountainous" or "tremendous" or "the worst I've ever seen." The fact is that in the beginning hours of a strong western gale on western Lake Erie the waves are generally at a maximum of about nine feet. Seas can get as high as 12 feet in some western areas, but a good average is about six to eight feet. The farther east that one travels on that lake, the higher the waves will get, but in the *Tasmania's* storm, it is likely that the seas were running in the six to nine foot range at her time and location. The hazard comes when you have a heavily laden vessel sitting low in the water plus the actions of her hull when placed into the rolling waves. In the case of the *Tasmania,* her hull was 221-feet in length. Additionally, in her era, there was no enforcement of any sort when it came to the loading of a schooner-barge. They were simply loaded to the point that their captain considered to be what the vessel could handle. Plus there was no authority what-so-ever to check the safe loading of a vessel. Knowing that, it is easy to imagine the *Tasmania* as being loaded to, or perhaps a bit beyond, her maximum safe capacity for a late autumn trip. Thus, being low in the water she would be an easy target for seas greater than five or six feet. A six foot sea boarding a vessel with just four feet of freeboard would run across the deck nearly hip deep on most crewmen. With post-shipwreck vision, a survivor may indeed easily describe such seas as being "tremendous" or even "mountainous" or perhaps "the worst I've ever seen."

In the storm, from the *Ashland* the dim amber lamps of the *Tasmania* were soon fading in and out as the squalls of rain and sleet obscured the view. The more numerous lamps of the steamer *Bulgaria* were only a bit better seen ahead. As the storm swept trio passed the Pelee Passage light, the time came to make the turn onto the course for the Southeast Shoal lightship and then direct to Cleveland. The course that the trio had been on since leaving the Detroit River was 095 degrees, or nearly due east, thus they were taking the seas on their sterns. Now, as the *Bulgaria* turned onto the more southerly course of 120 degrees, the seas were quartering on their beam ends. Before long Lake Erie was coming aboard the three vessels and dancing among their hatches. Taking water over their rails, the three lakers rolled and corkscrewed in Lake Erie's steep, sharp and frequent seas that came in rapid punches.

There is no clear record as to what happened next, as the only statement given by the master of the *Ashland* was that the *Tasmania* was having a bad time of it and "It was seen

CHRISTENED WITH WATER - INTERRED WITH DYNAMITE

Unable to make her run for shelter with the schooner-barge Tasmania *in tow, the steamer* Bulgaria *was forced to drop the barge and leave her to her own ends on a storm-swept Lake Erie. The* Bulgaria's *crew cut the towing hawser and never looked back.*
Photo Credit Don Comtois

that the line to the *Ashland* (from the *Tasmania*) must be cut." Thus a crewman went aft and severed the towing hawser to release the *Tasmania* from the rest of the tow. The lone newspaper account then paraphrases the eyewitness saying that "It seemed that she sunk at once." The time was five o'clock in the morning and the *Bulgaria,* with the *Ashland* in tow, proceeded to the lee of Pelee Island where they sheltered for more than 24 hours, waiting for conditions to moderate before heading on to Cleveland.

The *Tasmania* had indeed sunk, and likely went down quite quickly. The reason for her sinking was very simple - after 35 seasons of hard labor, the Great Lakes had finally stressed her timbers beyond the limits of their age and the workmanship put into her construction. Leaking beyond the capacity of her pumps, the boat simply plunged beneath the waves like a brick.

In looking closely at the wreck, however, a question comes up. The *Tasmania's* wreck itself is located two miles west of the course to Cleveland, some 15 degrees off the normal track. She is slightly less than 2 miles southwest of the Southeast Shoal lightship's former location and the wreck is reportedly sitting on the bottom pointed "west three quarters south" or nearly on a course toward Pelee Island rather than toward Cleveland. The boat's anchors were aboard her, so there was no effort to drop them and swing her into the wind. Pondering all of the elements, we can ask why this is her position?

Several answers can be composed, but the most likely would be that once passing the Southeast Shoal lightship, the *Bulgaria's* captain decided that his boat and her consorts could not handle the lake all the way into Cleveland and he took on the difficult task of turning nearly due west to run for Pelee Island. The *Tasmania's* location likely indicates that he made the turn successfully, but the wallowing maneuver must have taken a heavy toll on the two schooner-barges and perhaps even on the steamer itself. Once head to the wind and seas, however, the progress of the tow must have slowed to a snail's pace. Although coming aboard less, the seas now pounded the vessels with a greater intensity. It is likely that the master of the *Ashland* sensed that the *Tasmania's* storm drenched bulk was dragging his vessel down and thus cut her loose. If he ordered that done and the *Tasmania* plunged to the bottom shortly thereafter, he may indeed have saved his boat.

None of the eight crewmen aboard the *Tasmania* survived the wreck. Four days later the *Tasmania's* remains were

In spite of the hoodoo of being Christened with water, the James C. Couch *went on to a long career. However, she eventually ended her days as the* Tasmania *in a Lake Erie shipwreck. Photo Credit Ralph Roberts collection*

located by the United States tug *Spear* as part of an expedition mounted by United States Engineer William T. Blunt. The expedition measured 38.5 feet of water over the wreck. Blunt found the wreck site easy to locate as the *Tasmania's* masts were sticking well above the surface. No bodies of her crew were ever reported as being found nor is there any report of a search effort. In those days if your boat went down, you were simply considered lost with it unless you happened to show up otherwise. The following summer the Midland Towing and Wrecking Company was contracted by the Canadian government to flatten the wreck with dynamite because it was considered to be a hazard to navigation. Early in the summer of 1906 the demolition job was completed and the *Tasmania* was "cleared." She had been christened with water and now had been interred with dynamite. That should have closed the books on the story of the big schooner barge and what few of her original critics that were still alive were able to sit back and say "I told ya' so... no vessel christened with water can meet a happy ending." Yet, in spite of that self-fulfilling prophecy, the saga of the *Tasmania* had a new chapter written 82 years after her wreck.

Wreck-stripping divers from Ohio invaded the waters of the Sovran nation of Canada sometime during 1987. Their target was the wreck of the *Tasmania* and her huge wooden stock anchors. Using two boats, a lift-bag, and a hacksaw, they freed one anchor from the wreck and smuggled it back to the USA and their private storage facility. Upon learning of the theft, members of SOS (Save Ontario Shipwrecks) attempted to negotiate the return of the anchor to the wreck. The thieves refused and shortly thereafter found their storage facility raided by United States Customs and other law enforcement agencies. The wreck-looters had their warehouse contents, boats and other tools of their trade confiscated and then suffered greatly under additional legal actions. Meanwhile, SOS, along with the Canadian Coast Guard, returned the anchor to the *Tasmania's* grave - where it belongs.

FIRST OF THE DOOMED SISTERS

Author's note: This story was in my very first book Stormy Seas *written in 1986 and released in publication in 1991, and later reprinted in* Stormy Disasters *in 2001. In 2010, the main player in this story - the steamer L.R. Doty -reached out from the pages of history made modern headlines. For that reason I felt it necessary to update and republish the following story.*

THE first snow of the winter of 1898 came with the predawn hours of Tuesday, October 25. A storm front stretching as far south as the Gulf of Mexico pushed its way across the Great Lakes and without warning grew in intensity until by Tuesday morning a full gale was blowing. The worst storm in 25 years dumped thick wet snow across all of the Great Lakes. At Sheboygan, Wisconsin, a large group of townsfolk braved the weather to watch Lake Michigan's waves destroy over 100 feet of the Taylor dock. Cresting at nearly 12 feet, the ice cold breaking waves were rolling down from the northeast pushed by a north wind of over 70-miles per hour.

Around the Great Lakes, battered vessels hauled for shelter. Wallowing into Alpena came the Union Steamboat Company's powerful 340-feet steel freighter *Ramapo*. Rarely had this giant steamer been pounded into running from an angry lake, but on this storm-racked night the waves beating on the *Ramapo's* rudder had caused her steering chains to part. Without the service of her rudder, the big boat quickly fell off into the trough of the sea. The mountainous cresting waves began to take advantage of the steamer. Breaking in her cabins and washing through her galley, the icy lake carried away all the boat's provisions. Soon the *Ramapo's* crew rigged relieving tackles to the boat's rudder arm and the battered steamer ran for Alpena. Once there she joined a tiny fleet of boats sheltering there. The schooners *Demond*, *Hattie*, *William P. Fessenden*, and the steamer *Colonial* were all waiting out the storm in Alpena's sheltered waters. It was another story for the steel steamer *Republic*, that challenged Lake Huron's fury only to be thrown onto North Point like a hunk of driftwood.

At the Soo, the 432-feet steel steamer *Sir Henry Bessemer* hissed into the locks towing the 376-feet whaleback barge *Alexander Holley*. Both boats were downbound with bellies full of Marquette ore when they were overtaken by the storm. Rain turned quickly into ice pellets and the wind screamed down upon the two boats at nearly 65-miles per hour. With a resounding crack, the steel towline parted and the two boats drifted apart. The *Bessemer* made nine efforts to pick up the wayward pigboat during the frothing night. Finally the decision was made to stand by the barge until dawn on Tuesday morning. With the aid of dawn's light, a line was made fast between the two boats and they hauled for the Soo.

For nearly four days, from late Sunday night until early Thursday, the storm churned Lake Michigan. As early as Tuesday afternoon shipping had become a tangled mess. At Michigan City, the wooden steamer *H.A. Tuttle* laden with grain suddenly broke in half in the mouth of the river. She sat there for 20 hours with giant seas exploding over her broken hull before the lifesavers could remove her crew. The consort to the *Tuttle*, the 211-foot *Aberdeen*, was cut loose on the open lake before the steamer failed. Having been constructed at Bay City's Davidson yard in 1892, the *Aberdeen* was relatively new. Hopefully, she could hold her own against the storm. The schooner was last seen adrift on the raging open lake. Both boats were under control of the Minch Transit Company.

Milwaukee's harbor saw a sudden rush of storm-ravaged boats seeking shelter. Out of the maelstrom steamed the *Gogebic*, dropping both hooks in the harbor's protected waters. Missing was the *Gogebic's* consort, the wooden schooner barge *Pewabic*. The might of the storm had forced the steamer to drop her barge out on the open lake so that the *Gogebic* could turn and run for Milwaukee. The battered schooner was left to her own ends and was last seen drifting near Sheboygan. Running for shelter came the schooner *Mabel Wilson*, but a giant cresting wave struck her short of safety and slammed the boat into the breakwater. Luckily for the wind-grabber, the lake delivered only a glancing blow and the wounded schooner limped into calm waters. The schooner *Barbarian*, who had dropped her hooks in the bay off Milwaukee during the night, was suffering damage at her stern, but seemed to be riding well. Out on the open lake off Racine, Wisconsin, the 161-foot schooner *D.L. Filer* was sighted adrift with her sails blown out and masts down. The Racine Lifesavers aided by the tug *Dixon*, beat their way out to the drifting schooner and successfully removed her crew.

Port Huron became the safe haven for vessels smart enough not to challenge a roaring Lake Huron. Returning to the shelter of the St. Clair River came the tug *Torrent*, followed by the steel steamer *Niagara*. The *Mercer*, *Sweepstakes*, *Douglas*, *John Oads*, *Havana*, *Stephenson*, *Coriliss* and *Centurion* all put out lines at Port Huron. The boats coming in off the tossing lake joined a crowd of vessels who were already tucked snugly in the bright blue river.

ALL HANDS ON DECK

Among the fleet squatting out the storm were the steamers *Pontiac, Saginaw, Newaygo, Choctaw, W.D. Rees, Norton, Fayette Brown, Lagonda, Kearsarge, Crescent City,* and *Onoko.* Also sheltering at Port Huron was the *Presque Isle, John Duncan, India, Conemaugh, Charlie Crawford.* Rounding out Port Huron's roll-call of sheltered boats were the *Boston, Arabian, Laura Wesley, Wade, Shenandoah, Crete,* and *Hadley.* Near the height of the storm, the crews of all the sheltered boats were quite astonished to see the steamer *Bangor* steam passively upbound into the wild lake. Her master, looking back at the protected fleet, probably gave a deep "harumph" and mumbled, "lose a day because of a little weather...not by a damn sight."

Late into Wednesday night, the wind howled and the snow and sleet blew horizontally. By the first hours of Thursday morning, the wind died suddenly and the vessel communities around the lakes began the anxious wait for the weather-mauled boats to return to port. 1898 was in the era of massive shipping on the lakes, yet was also the age of telegraph communication at best. In a three-day gale of hurricane magnitude, the fragile telegraph lines were the first victims. The best source of information then became eyewitness accounts and rumors.

At Cleveland, the yacht *Cygnet* had been beaten to pieces while, at Alpena, the *Republic* floated free of North Point eventually limping into port. For some reason, however, Lake Michigan seemed to be the hardest hit. At Chicago, the schooner *Delta* was tugged in with her spars blown down. Along the city's lake front more than 81,000 dollars in damage had been done by the wind and waves. Wrecked outside of Chicago Harbor, the schooner *Aloha* had settled to the lake bottom. Off Racine, Wisconsin, the abandoned schooner *D.L. Filer* was recovered and towed into port.

120

FIRST OF THE DOOMED SISTERS

Those anxiously waiting for word of the missing schooner barge *Pewabic* were reassured to hear that she had been brought into Sheboygan with her spars, sails, anchors and deck equipment gone, but her crew in good condition. Also safe were the crewmembers of the steamer *Tuttle* which had gone completely to pieces at Michigan City.

In the first hours of Thursday, October 27, 1898, the steamer *Louisville* found the weather safe enough to push her way out of Chicago bound for St. Joseph, Michigan. At 7:00, Captain Boswell of the *Louisville* sighted a battered schooner rolling sluggishly in the cold gray dawn. Although several miles distant, he could still identify the stricken schooner barge as the *Olive Jeanette*. Passing closer to the schooner, the *Louisville* crew could see that the *Jeanette's* masts had been blown down and her rudder had been carried away. Although damaged, she did not appear to be in danger. So assured of the schooner's condition was the *Louisville's* captain that he steamed right past her and continued to St. Joseph. Upon arrival there, Captain Boswell wired Chicago reporting the approximate position of the drifting schooner and two tugs were promptly dispatched to recover the *Olive Jeanette*.

After making her lines fast to a south Chicago dock the *Jeanette's* master, Captain D.B. Cadotte, told those ashore the story of his boat's brush with disaster. The schooner barge had departed south Chicago early Monday afternoon in tow of the wooden steamer *L.R. Doty*. Both boats were upbound with cargoes of grain consigned to Midland, Ontario, far into Lake Huron's Georgian Bay. For nearly 24 hours the two boats battled their way into the intensifying gale. Then at five o'clock Tuesday evening, off Milwaukee, the tow line parted and the *Jeanette* fell off into the trough of the wild seas. Captain Cadotte watched as the *Doty* continued northward, head to the seas. Into the blowing sleet the big steamer slowly faded. Captain Cadotte figured that she would make a wide circle, returning to pick his boat up, but he knew too well that there would be little chance of turning the big steamer in this kind of sea.

Figuring that he was on his own, Captain Cadotte ordered the *Olive Jeanette's* sails rigged. It was his good fortune that the boat was stocked with brand new canvas and as soon as it was raised, he ran for Racine, Wisconsin. For the better part of five hours the barge showed the storm her heels with the giant cresting seas slamming at her stern. Then shortly after eleven o'clock an angry wave broke her steering gear. The wind in her sails pulled the boat around into the trough of the heaving seas once again. As the barge's desperate crew scurried to make repairs to the steering gear, thundering seas repeatedly crashed aboard her decks. Soon everything on her decks, including her steam pumps and deckhouse, had been swept away. Somehow the sailors managed to re-rig the rudder tackles and the wooden schooner barge again ran before the seas. By this time, however, the boat had been blown south of Racine, being unable to turn northward into the wind. Captain Cadotte had no choice other than running south for Chicago nearly 70 miles down the churning lake.

Hours later, the *Olive Jeanette* had worked only a fraction of the distance to Chicago when an enraged Lake Michigan again lashed out at the barge once again. This time the schooner's giant oak rudder was bitten from her stern and with it her ability to steer was completely destroyed. Through skillful manipulation of the boat's sails alone, Captain Cadotte was able to keep out of the sea trough and remain before the wind. Shortly before dawn, what should have been the death stroke came. A violent series of wind gusts burst over the boat, blasting her sails to shreds. From that moment on, the *Jeanette* was left to wallow in the trough of the killer

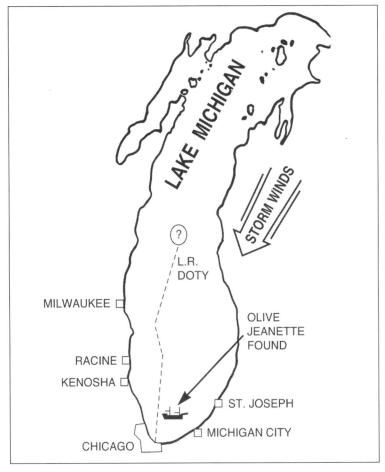

seas. At daybreak Thursday, when the storm lifted the schooner was still afloat. Her hatches had saved her. For some unexplainable reason the hatch canvas had remained tightly sealed through the whole ordeal and barely a drop of water had found its way into her cargo.

As Captain Cadotte told his story he stopped for a moment to inquire as to the *L.R. Doty's* port of shelter. Surely the giant, five year old, wooden steamer had found a cozy port along the north shore and would by now be pushing her way south to recover the *Olive Jeanette*. After all her captain, Christopher Smith, was not one to leave loose ends unattended to. Not a man along the dock had heard of the *Doty's* location. The real concern had been for the *Olive Jeanette* and a news release was promptly telegraphed off to the *West Bay City Tribune*. It read: "...The schooner *Olive Jeanette* was picked up off Kenosha, Wis. and brought into Chicago with all canvas and the rudder gone after weathering the gale Tuesday night. The schooner was separated from its consort, the steamer *Doty*, somewhere in Lake Michigan. The *Doty* is still out in the lake. Both boats are partially fitted with crews from this city." As the type-setter's fingers busily laid the letters of the story in the cluttered *Tribune* office, a much larger story was being written on the heaving surface of Lake Michigan as the steam tug *Prodigy* suddenly found herself pushing through a giant field of churning wreckage. By late Thursday afternoon, the *Prodigy* was tied up at the Chicago Independent Tug Line's dock. Captain Ebison of the steamer *George Williams* of the Hawgood Line, which also owned the *Doty*, was performing the grim task of identifying the wreckage that the *Prodigy* had brought in off the lake.

The *L.R. Doty* was actually being run by the Cuyahoga Transit Company, but at this point there was no use in debating whose colors she had been flying from her foremast; all that remained were bits of flotsam. It was in search of the *Olive Jeanette* that the *Prodigy* had been dispatched, but when the tug was 25 miles off Kenosha, Wisconsin, she came upon a large field of wreckage. At first the tug's crew thought they had found the *Olive Jeanette's* death smudge, but it soon became apparent that these were the remains of a giant wooden steamer. Cabin doors veneered with mahogany were the final clue. These, along with a large chunk of oak deck, told those on the *Prodigy* that one of the big, new, wooden steamers had met her fate. The tug brought the doors, some stanchions and a pole that was painted the brown color of the *Doty's* hull, into the Chicago office where Captain Ebison, who had sailed the *Doty*, quickly identified them as being from the *L.R. Doty*. Finally, to further seal the case of the *L.R. Doty*, she was the only boat on Lake Michigan that was unaccounted for.

In 1892, the F. W. Wheeler shipyard at West Bay City began work on the 201-foot hull of the *L.R. Doty*. Over 50 acres of white oak trees were consumed in the construction of the giant steamer. When she splashed off the builder's ways into the Saginaw River, the *Doty* carried an insurance rating of A-l, with a star. Her owners insisted that she be equipped with the best lifeboat that money could buy. Five years later, she carried both to the bottom of Lake Michigan in the blink of an eye.

Perhaps it was her family that was doomed from the start. You see, the *L.R. Doty* was one of six sisters, most of whom came to grief on the lakes. Duplicates of the *Doty* were the *Uganda*, and *William F. Sauber*. Also sisters to the *Doty* were the *Tampa*, which was rammed and sunk on the Detroit River in 1911, then later returned to service. Finally there was the ghost ship *Iosco*, which vanished on Lake Superior September 3, 1905. Coincidentally, it would be the *Iosco* who took the *Olive Jeanette* to eternity with her on that stormy day. The schooner had survived the fate of one of the doomed sisters, only to "sail away" with another. Of the five sisters from the F. W. Wheeler Yard only one, the *C.F. Bielman*, survived to work out a productive career.

On Friday evening, October 28, 1898, the *Bay City Times-Press* carried the grim news. "The *L.R. Doty* feared she has gone to the bottom." The same article listed the names of those thought to be gone with the Bay City boat. Captain

Christopher Smith, Chief Thomas Abernethie, Mate Henry Sharpe, Second Mate W.J. Hossie, Second Engineer C.W. Odette, Oiler George Wadkin, Watchman Charles Bornie, Wheelsmen Peter G. Peterson and Albert Nelson, Firemen Joseph Fitzsimon and John Howe, Deckhands F. Harmuth, C. Curtis, William Ebart, and Pat Ryan, Cook W.J. Scott, and finally Steward Lawrence E. Goss, who resided at 203 Prairie Av. in West Bay City.

Over a century later the events of that stormy week have been mostly forgotten and the eyewitnesses to the gale are long dead. Of all the lakeboats that weathered the storm, only the *E.M. Ford*, which was formerly the *Presque Isle* is, as of this writing, still floating upon the water of the lakes. The *Ford*, however, as of 2010, sits laid-up in a Canadian scrap yard slip, waiting for the prices of scrap to climb enough to justify putting the torch to her. Yet, in the year 2010, from the depths of Lake Michigan, the *L.R. Doty* would reach up from her ice water grave and write national headlines once again.

Exactly how that happened has to do with modern technology in both electronic detection aids and deep water scuba diving. It also has a lot to do with a somewhat new generation of Great Lakes research historians. This is a group that believes that tall tales and dramatic yarns of lakeboats and shipwrecks are fine for dull nights in the pilothouse on the open lake or around the campfire ashore, but the search and discovery of lost factual history is far more captivating and important. For persons of this ilk, each event in Great Lakes maritime history represents a case of ultimate detective work and if that research opens as many new questions as it answers, that alone means you are doing it right. This leads to more investigation and discovery and it is that same process of discovery that makes the effort worthwhile. Among the foremost in this new generation of research

FIRST OF THE DOOMED SISTERS

In her career on the lakes, the big wooden oreboat L.R. Doty *was considered to be one of the finest examples of the shipbuilder's craft. Then came the day she battled with Lake Michigan's fury. She is seen here locking upbound with what is believed to be her consort* Olive Jeanette. *Courtesy of the Great Lakes Historical Society*

historians is one of the most tenacious history detectives on the Great Lakes - Brendon Baillod. With his help, a team of the very determined "technical divers" would find the resting place of the long lost *L.R. Doty*.

Since the exact location of the final resting place of the *Doty* was never known, she had always been known as just another "ghost ship" of the Great Lakes. The old mariners often referred to such lost vessels as having "sailed through a crack in the lake." Of course, the new generation of research historians accepts that adage, then goes looking for the crack. There are often clues and more often false trails that lead to such a wreck's gravesite and the *Doty* was no exception. Many times when someone would stumble upon what they considered to be a "large" wreck or piece of what they thought to be a "large" wreck, someone would try and attach the *Doty* to the site. For nearly a century these leads always turned out not to have anything to do with the *L.R. Doty*. The problem being that the *Doty* was not a "large" wooden vessel, but rather she was a "giant" wooden vessel. Anyone who stumbled upon her would surely know it without any doubt.

A clue to the location of the wreck came in the late summer of 1991 when a fishing tug snagged its gill net on a deeply submerged object. The fisherman reported the snag to a Milwaukee dive charter captain who went to that location and charted the object using a fish-finder. Although he had no way of knowing it for sure, the charter captain had just charted one of the lakes' long lost shipwrecks - the *L.R. Doty*. It appeared to be a very large object in more than 300 feet of water. In 1991, however, the technology needed to dive that deep was not widely used by the divers who would pay to have the charter captain take them out. Since the site was outside of his market and the distance to the site, some 20 miles off shore, was prohibitive, the good charter captain simply noted the site and then went back to doing practical business.

Sometime in the mid-1990s, the charted object caught the attention of Brendon Baillod. He began the mental and paper process of elimination and detective work that comes naturally to a research historian and directed his efforts toward the identification of the object. For a decade and a half the object was on Baillod's "wonder who" list. Although there were several significant vessels that may be the object, no divers could be motivated to make the long trip out to the site. Technology, however, would soon seed the motivation needed to find and document the object.

As the century turned, the sport of "technical diving" began to become more affordable and thus more common among serious scuba divers. Involving the use of mixed gasses and rebreathers, technical diving allows an advanced diver to go to great depths with no ill effects. One of the people at the heart of this new era of deep diving is Milwaukee charter captain Jitka Hanakova. Since Brendon

FIRST OF THE DOOMED SISTERS

Baillod had worked with Jitka on several other shipwrecks, he approached her at the 2009 Milwaukee Ghost Ships Festival with the idea of locating and exploring the deep object and they agreed to give it a try in 2010. In May of that year, they went out and after a protracted search, found the object's location.

Accompanied by technical divers John Janzen, Lubo Valuch, Tracy Xelowski, Ron Benson and another diver, as well as historian, Peter Scotland, Brendon Baillod and Captain Hanakova headed out in search of that crack in the lake. It was just after 10 o'clock on the morning June 16, 2010, as the first three divers descended into the depths. After a protracted period they sent up a message "all divers ok... up in 80 minutes... huge wooden steamship." Brendon knew instinctively from that message what the video would later confirm beyond doubt; they had found the long lost *L.R. Doty* and were now anchored over the grave of her crew.

Resting with her hull intact, the *Doty* squats in the mud at the bottom of Lake Michigan. Piles of that mud have been shoveled onto her stern deck by the action of her impacting stern-first into the lakebed. Her smoke stack lays on its side, ripped from her engine room roof, yet seeming unwilling to leave her. Her hatches yawn wide open to the lake, their covers having been blown off by air trapped in the hull as she took her death plunge. Between two hatches, a wheelbarrow sits, as if waiting for a ghostly crew member to come and use it to trim her load. Overall, the entire wreck is covered in a blanket of Quagga mussels that cling to everything. To humanity, although the wreck may be a tragic marker of a storm that is nearly forgotten, the *L.R. Doty* is now no longer lost. In today's world of the Great Lakes shipwreck historian, there are no vessels that disappeared, they are all down there somewhere.

A PEEK INSIDE THE BLODGETT FLEET

ALTHOUGH the lumber industry had been in decline for nearly 20 years, the era of the wooden ship came to a very sudden end with the on-set of the Great Depression. All around the lakes small fleets of wooden steamers and their schooner-barge consorts had been a common sight since the middle of the 1800s. Bulk cargoes of all sorts, from lumber to iron ore, were hauled around the Great Lakes in this fashion. Yet in a single mass extinction, shipping in that configuration by that sort of vessel was wiped from the face of the fresh water seas following the stock market crash of 1929. In every single backwater around the lakes, once useful wooden vessels of all sizes were simply abandon and left to rot as their operating companies vanished. Steel lakeboats were also left to rust, but as the first years of the depression dragged on, the steel hulls stood up much better to idle time than did the wooden hulls. As World War II pulled the industrial base out of the decline, the wooden ships were all too far gone to be of any use. The wooden ship's time had expired forever.

One such fleet that was making a fair living in the declining years of the wooden lakeboat was that of Omer W. Blodgett. Based in Bay City, Michigan, the Blodgett fleet consisted of fine wooden lumber hookers and schooner-barges, all in the later years of their life. Still, the fleet was well maintained and sporting their trademark white strip the length of their hulls, they were a well recognized group of lakeboats in the early 1900s. Much of what it was really like to live and work in such fleets has long been lost as the people directly involved have passed on. Yet we are very lucky to have access to that world by means of a letter composed by Omer W. Blodgett's grandson, Omer William Blodgett. In that letter he gives us a candid look into what it was like growing up with the Blodgett fleet as well as how the era of the wooden lakeboat came to an end. His letter is transcribed here - so small grammatical edits have been made and some "author's notes" have been added in order to provide context. Still, he gives us a fascinating look into a time that can never be repeated.

"Our grandfather Omer W Blodgett (on my father's side) was born and raised in Kingsville, Ohio, a tiny village about 40 miles east of Cleveland. He was born on a farm and his folks also did tanning. He taught school when he was 18 years old. He did not want to farm all his life so he went sailing on the boats on the Great Lakes as a purser. This was in the days before telegraph and telephone so the owner would have a purser who operated the tow (steamboat and 2 to 4 barges) for him, getting a cargo to be shipped, paying off the crew etc. Grandpa worked hard, saved his money and at the height of his career he owned about 23 ships, steamboats and barges. At the last he had two steel boats, the Kiowa *and the* Cayuga. *I believe they were built in World War I as Liberty Ships.* (*Author's note: The *Kiowa* and *Cayuga* were both Frederickstadt type three island vessels constructed for World War I use on the high seas - they were still on the builder's ways when the war ended and were purchased as war surplus. Both vessels fell under the ownership of the Independent Steamship Company of Duluth. In 1927 they were transferred to the management of Blodgett, but each vessel was registered as its own company. Thus the *Kiowa*

A PEEK INSIDE THE BLODGETT FLEET

Entertainment on the twice-annual trips between Duluth and Bay City could be as simple as a board. Here two of the Blodgett girls are seen having fun on a make-shift teeter-totter using nothing more than a hatch strongback and the boom from the forward mast. Photo Credit Blodgett family

because the Kiowa Transportation Company and the *Cayuga* became the Cayuga Transportation Company.) *He began loading lumber in Bay City area when lumber was taken and shipped east by boat. When the timber was depleted there, they pushed further north and began taking timber out of Duluth, Minnesota, about the year 1900.*

From late spring to fall we would be up at Duluth, Minnesota. Dad would be busy getting the boats in and out of port. When the boats got up to Duluth or Superior, a steam boat with three or four barges, they would split up for unloading and later for loading. They might have brought up limestone; if so, they would unload at Cuttler Magner in Duluth. They might have brought up salt; if so, they would unload at Cuttler Magner salt dock in Duluth or Morton Salt dock in Superior. When unloaded, they would go to another dock and load pulp wood. This all took time. A steam engine would back a long string of railway cars called gondolas down onto the dock. Sometime during the day as these cars were unloaded, it would be necessary for the engine to return to the dock and pull the empty rail cars out and replace them with loaded cars. This was very time consuming, especially when there was a problem in getting a switch engine down to the docks. This was a problem many times. Not only did the steam boat have to be loaded but frequently it had to go to a different dock to pick up the loaded barges. Sometimes the steam boat was loaded in Duluth and went across the harbor to Superior and picked up other barges. Eventually the steam boat would fuel (pick up coal for the trip down the lakes), then pick up the remaining barges (the tow) and leave port to head down Lake Superior to deliver the pulp wood to a paper mill.

Seen here in 1932 the last boat in the Blodgett fleet, the Grampian *is laid up in the company's "swamp." Later she would be towed to the Davidson yard for servicing and then abandoned there. Photo Credit Author's collection*

A PEEK INSIDE THE BLODGETT FLEET

Some of the pulp wood would be collected during the winter at a location along the shore. This could be Knife River, Two Harbors, Grand Marais, and sometimes along the shore of Lake Superior miles from nowhere. The boats would anchor at this area. A flat scow with a boom and hoist, called an unloader, would tie up beside the boat to be loaded. Its boom would extend out over the hold of the boat to be loaded. A steel cable would be run ashore, pass through a large pulley or shieve fastened on the shore near the pulp wood. The steel cable would be returned to the boom of the unloader. A large quantity of pulp wood would be put together and a hook from this cable would be attached to the pulp wood. The unloader would reel in the cable, causing the bundle of pulp wood to be pulled up by the boom and over to the opening of the ship, then lowered into the hold of the boat. Once the pulp wood was released, several men in the hold would spread the load out into a smooth layer with a tool called a pickaxe. It was similar to an axe but with a point, allowing the "longshoreman" to line up the pieces of pulp wood in an orderly pattern. I was never at the other end of the lakes to see how the pulp wood was unloaded, but I assume it was some sort of a conveyor.

I first remember going to Grand Marais when I was very small, perhaps just a few years old. I remember waking up during the night and hearing the sound of a gasoline engine which drove a generator to supply the small city with electric power. It was one of those old engines that had a speed governor which would cut off the ignition when the speed was too great, then upon slowing down would allow it to start up again. It sounded like "putt-putt—-putt-putt-putt-putt——putt-putt—-" Whenever I woke up I could hear this. There was no other noise out there during the night. I remember the hotel was at least two stories in height. It must have been the old "Tourist Hotel," which burned down a long time ago.

In its final resting place the schooner-barge Grampian *sits in the early 1950s, sunken, where it was abandoned just outside of the gates to the Davidson Drydock in West Bay City in 1932. Photo Credit Ralph Roberts collection*

Our steam boat and at least one barge would anchor within the harbor in Grand Marais. I believe the pulp wood was floating on the water, contained by a chain of logs. Men with long pike poles would feed the logs into a conveyor which would carry them by a belt up and over the side of the boat from where they would drop into the hold of the boat.

I am not sure when we first loaded pulp wood at Grand Marais. I am sure we stopped loading there by 1928 or 1929.

Our folks used to live in both Bay City, Michigan and Duluth, Minnesota. When the season of navigation was over, somewhere in late October or early November we would move down to Bay City and live on one of the steam boats while they repaired the boats.

They would tie the boats up on the Saginaw River in Bay City, Michigan just south or upstream from the Midland Street bridge or Third Street bridge, on the west side of the river.

Soon after the boats arrived, marine inspectors from Port Huron would arrive and inspect the boats and lay out the required repair work for the winter months so they would be able to sail next season, damaged timber and planks replaced with new members. Seams had to be made water tight again by driving oakum into them and then pouring tar on top of the seam. This oakum was loosely twisted hemp impregnated with tar.

Frequently repair work had to be done on the boiler on the steam boats. They used a scotch marine boiler with fire tubes. The lower portion of the boiler contained the fire box, holding the hot coals of the fire. Water was contained in the boiler directly above the fire box. The flame passed backward along the fire box and passed upward at the end of the boiler and then passed forward through steel tubes or pipes and out up the stack.

The steam engine was a triple expansion engine. High pressure steam would enter the first cylinder, about 18 inches in diameter. The steam would then enter the second larger cylinder, about 28 inches in diameter. The steam would then enter the third larger cylinder about 36 to 40 inches in diameter. The diameter of the piston and cylinder was increased as the steam pressure decreased so that the connecting rod from the piston applied about the same force on the crank shaft. Later in early spring the marine inspectors would come in from Port Huron and give the boats their final inspection, checking the work which had been done during the winter. They would stay at the Winona Hotel, on the east side of Saginaw River in Bay City.

*Rather than firing up the boiler to test it, they would bring
a tug, called the witch alongside the steam boat and pipe high
pressure steam from the tug into the boiler of the boat. The
crews would arrive, supplies put on and the tows so they
could leave. A tow was made up of one steam boat and three
or four barges. The tow would take the name of the steam
boat, for example "the Bradley tow". They would split up
when they arrived in port, going sometimes to different docks,
but getting together again upon loading and leaving port.*

*Our family would live on board one of the steam boats
during the winter. This was called "keeping ship." One of
our barges, the* Marion W. Page, *had been in an accident and
lost her bow section.* (*Author's note: an "accident" such as
the one described here took place on October 1, 1915 when
the *Page* collided with the 400-foot steamer *George B.
Leonard* in the Saint Clair Flats at the southern mouth of the
Saint Clair River. That accident, however, pre-dates the era
of this account by about five years. As of this writing, no
record of another similar and later accident has been found.)
*She had been towed into Bay City and docked along side of
what we called the "swamp" on the west side of the river,
just directly south of the Midland Street Bridge. This bridge
collapsed a few years ago and was not replaced* (*Author's
note: the Third Street bridge collapsed on the night of June
18, 1976, after swinging open for the sand-sucker *Niagara*.)
*This street was called Third Street on the east side of the river
and Midland Street on the west side. The swamp was later
made into a park after we left (after 1931). Grandfather built
a two story, square wood building on the foreward portion of
the* Page. *The lower or first floor contained quite a bit of
wood working machinery, about three desks, the rest of the
floor was used to repair chipping guns, riveting guns, air
reamer, etc. There was also a smaller one story wooden*

building containing a very large Chicago pneumatic air compressor and later a Lincoln 200 ampere electric arc welder, purchased in 1917. Our Swedish watchman, Nels Turner, lived by himself in the cabin at the aft end of the Page.

When the boats were tied up for the winter in Bay City, there was a space of about ten feet between them. Spanned by a gang plank, this was made of an old hatch cover, with a railing added on each side so we would not fall off. This space between the boats allowed scaffolding to be placed along the side of the boat for repairs.

We had a walkway from the Third Street sidewalk to the first boat, the Page. *This walk was also made of old hatch covers and was elevated about two feet above the swamp, because the swamp sometimes flooded in the spring.*

Following a collision with the steamer George B. Leonard *in 1915 the bow of the* Marion W. Page, *seen here, was completely severed. She never sailed again. The* Page *was subsequently taken to the Blodgett Company's "swamp" where a two story repair shop was constructed on her deck and the boat became a floating workshop.*
Photo Credit Blodgett family

ALL HANDS ON DECK

Loading pulpwood aboard the steamer Charles H. Bradley *and the schooner-barge* Grampian. *Photo Credit Blodgett family*

When we "kept ship" during the winter, we lived in the aft section where most of the crew would have stayed. This consisted of a large dining room in the central portion. A portion of the roof was raised about 1 1/2 feet above the rest of the roof to form a "sky light". This section contained glass around the four sides, to allow day light to enter this room. On some boats, colored glass was used. We removed the large dining table and made this room into our living room. We had a small table along one side from which we ate, and after supper, we three children studied our lessons, using a single table lamp. Most steam boats had a large built in "side board", with a large mirror and many small shelves to hold dishes, this was at the foreward end of the room. At the aft end of the room, we set up an old pot belly cast iron coal fired stove. This was our only source of heat.

Mother cooked in the kitchen, just off of the dining room, on the port side. She used the ship's stove, which was coal fired. Nels kept her supplied with coal, but she had to keep the range going and cook or bake at the same time. My mother's only fear was that one of us would fall off and drown in the river. Fortunately this never happened.

Around the dining room were several rooms or cabins which also opened outward to the deck along the side of the boat. These cabins had built in bunks. My brother and I shared one cabin. He slept in the lower bunk and I was fortunate enough to have the upper bunk. Dad would get up about 5 AM in the morning and build the fire.

When the navigational season started some time during May, the boats would leave. We would move over to my grandmother's (and grandfather's) house on the east side and stay there for a short time until we went up to Duluth. This always happened before school was out, so we missed some school. Upon arriving in Duluth, we would not enter school until the Fall. During the summer my father and grandfather would be busy keeping the boats moving without delay. They could only get so many round trips in during the season. My father once said that the last trip for a tow (about 6) would be the profit for the year. If they missed this last trip, there would be no profit. When the season of navigation ended, (this was tied into the length of time they were insured) we would return to Bay City leaving sometime after Thanksgiving. This again meant leaving school in Duluth before the term was over and we would not enter the Bay City school until the term started after Christmas. This we did, year after year until I was 12 years old, 1929. I was born in Duluth, November 27, 1917. They held off going down to Bay City until I was born.

This shipping business declined during the depression around 1929. The Kiowa *went down off Whitefish Point with a load of flax in 1929, I believe in November,* (*Author's note: the exact date was November 30.) *during a very bad storm.*

I was with my father and my brother, John, on the Kiowa *in Duluth the night she left Duluth. The captain was Alex T. Young, who had married my Aunt May. The chief engineer was a good friend of my father. When my father went down to see that the* Kiowa *got out of port, we found these two men were in a very heated argument, and neither would leave port with the other. My father had a real problem because the weather was getting bad and he had to get the ship out of Duluth. He finally separated the men and asked the chief engineer to sail with the captain as a personal favor. The* Kiowa *did leave but a couple of days later ran into a bad Northeaster. The cargo shifted and the ship started to sink. The captain ordered all hands into lifeboats. Only the captain and the cook got into a lifeboat and into the stormy seas. The crew remained on the* Kiowa. *The lifeboat rolled over, but the captain and the cook were able to right it and get back in. They drifted off and eventually drowned. They were the only ones lost. About a day later the Coast Guard got the crew off.*

Several weeks later we made our usual trip to Bay City, Michigan, where our boats would tie up for the winter to be repaired. Aunt May, who had just lost her husband, had moved in with my grandparents in Bay City. We kids had heard of a new movie called "Twenty Thousand Leagues Under the Sea" by Jules Verne. My father, thinking a good movie would divert Aunt May's mind from this tragedy, brought her to see it not knowing it was a hair raising story of a submarine which sinks in deep water and there are all kinds of creatures down there including a very large octopus. Aunt May sat on the edge of her seat during the movie and my father was worried that she would get hysterical and start screaming. Well, we made it through the movie and my father later let us know that our idea was not very good.

I believe the Cayuga *went back to the American Ship Co. and was later sold to a Hungarian company. Both of these*

The Page *is seen here in the background behind the schooner-barge* Brightie. *Photo Credit Blodgett family*

ships had the engine midship. Their masts were square in cross section instead of round and were called kingposts. (*Author's note: *Kiowa* reverted to her original ownership under the Independent Steamship Company in 1931 and was sold for off-lakes use in 1937 to Panamanian registry. The following year she sank in a storm after striking a shoal off of St. Ives, England. All but 3 of her crew survived.)

My father expected to work with my grandfather. After graduating from high school, he entered the Civil Engineering Department of the University of Michigan and graduated in 1910. He told us that he took civil engineering because he felt at that time he would get more basic engineering than in any other field.

We had steam boats and cargoes. When my father was a boy these "barges" were three masted schooners, with a full set of sails and a bow sprit sticking out of the bow. The masts were "stepped"; that is they were two spars in height, joined half way up.

Our last two ships, the steam boat Charles H. Bradley *and the barge* Grampian, *ended their days in the fall of 1931. I was attending East Junior High at the time and I remember the night my father got the phone call at home. They were coming into the Portage River Entry, Lake Superior, when the* Bradley *went aground because one of the channel lights was out. The* Grampian *ran into the stern of the* Bradley *and caused a fire. The* Bradley *burned to the water's edge. The* Grampian *was about to get away unharmed.* (*Author's note: the exact date of the *Bradley's* burning was October 9, 1931. The *Grampian* did manage to make her way back to Bay City, where she was then laid up, forever. After being laid up at the Blodgett "swamp" for several months, she was towed from the foot of the Third Street bridge in 1932 for a "servicing" at the Davidson yard. She was the last vessel ever serviced at the Davidson Shipyard as it officially went out of business when she was finished. At that same time, the *Grampian* was abandon by her owners and left to rot - the Blodgett fleet was no more. Her hulk rested on the west side of the river just south of the Veteran's Bridge until May 11, 1954, when vandals set fire to it and she burned to the waterline. In the mid-1990s, the last of her bones were dug out of the riverbank by the city.)

With the boat business gone, we could not operate with just a barge, Dad brought some machinery, including our welding machine up to Duluth where we were living at the time. We took our family car, a Reo, and put the welding machine in the back and connected it with a silent chain drive to the

*engine and we were in business. Later we rented a two story
wood building at 315 East Superior St. for $35.00 a month.
We later bought the building.*

*Our Aunt Alice, a daughter of O.W. Blodgett, my
grandfather, told me of one steamboat which had been
wrecked. The insurance company paid the claim to my
grandfather as they considered her a total loss. My
grandfather then went up to the wreck with some men during
the winter, repaired her and floated her off in the Spring. I don't
know if this was the* Mark Hopkins, *but it sounded like the one
you mentioned where no lives were lost and she was refloated.*

*My father had a second telephone in our home in Duluth,
in his bedroom. I remember on several occasions, the phone
ringing late at night or in the early hours of morning, telling
Dad that a boat had been lost. We could tell by the tone of
father's voice that it was serious. His first question was
always, "Was anyone lost?".*

*One of his worst ordeals was having to identify 18 bodies
washed ashore from the* Myron *which had been lost with all
hands except the captain. He had known these men personally.*

*Fortunately my grandfather had a hobby of taking pictures
of the boats as far back as 1900. I have some of his glass
negatives from which I have made prints. Some pictures show
the three masted schooners under sail.*

*In about 2 weeks Dorothy and I plan to go to Duluth and
then up along the highway along the lake to Grand Marais."*

I have no doubt that Omer and Dorothy Blodgett made that
trip up north and that every glimpse of the lakes along the
way brought back fond memories. From the pulpwood being
loaded to the steamer's galley converted to a living room, to
gas powered generator at Grant Marais that went "putt, putt—
—-putt——-putt, putt" it was all there in the fine time
machine called the human memory. Thanks to Omar's

memory, as well as his letter, we can all now share in those moments that would otherwise be lost to history. We can all spend a short time with the Blodgett family and the fleet of lake vessels that were the family business.

13 HATS

IN our time, if an entrepreneur needs to travel and if their personal time is considered to be of great value, they rarely depend on the modes of transportation used by the common public. Buses, trains, cars and airlines do not provide efficient enough transportation for persons of high stature or those who need to "get there and get back - now." They need to go directly to where they need to go without any delay or intermediate stops and often, money is no object. Such executive travelers charter private jets to speed them along their way to doing business and making money. These small airliners have small crews but they also have a focused obligation to their passengers. They eliminate all of the ticket counters, traffic jams and waiting in terminals. You pay, you get aboard and you go - period.

Most things were vastly different back in 1835, yet in a way, for one man something was very much the same. Although we do not know a lot about this man, he has left us with some interesting questions more than 165 years after his boots clomped along the waterfront of Kingston, Ontario. This individual, it seems, was traveling the route of a person who was doing important business. He needed to get where he needed to go without any delay or intermediate stops. With that thought in mind, he went down to the water front to charter a private schooner to take him to his destination. In short order this man of critical business had chartered the little schooner *Robert Bruce* along with her captain and small crew. Money was no object for the business man. After going aboard and paying Captain Ben Chandler, the business man still had $719 in cash in his coat pocket, the equivalent today of $15,155 Canadian dollars. Most historical accounts attach the business man with the name of Elias Everett, yet that moniker will weave a mystery that survives more than a century and a half after the man boarded the *Robert Bruce*.

Territory around the Great Lakes in 1835 was still largely wilderness. Canadian towns such as Toronto were only beginning to evolve into cities. A youthful Welland Canal, just half dozen years old, was in its infancy and was providing small schooners the chance to transit directly from Lake Ontario to the upper lakes. Any journey to the north and the west was the adventure of a lifetime and many times meant the end of a lifetime. Although the town of Buffalo had already become a bustling debarkation point of pioneers headed up the lakes, towns such as Detroit had not yet claimed their status as a city. Detroit itself was still finding its roots in the soil of Michigan whose statehood was still more than a year away. If the adventurer decided to proceed onward they would find the route lined with dense forests and unpopulated shores. The Mackinac straits were guarded by Fort Michilimackinac and its garrison of uniformed soldiers. From the straits down to Chicago the adventurer would, however, find more maritime activity than expected. Small villages were popping up all along both shores of Lake Michigan. All of these tiny towns relied on the lake for transportation, supplies and survival. The end point for the westward bound pioneer would be the town of Chicago and the fastest, best way to get there was by water.

Other than the name there was little about Chicago in 1835 that resembled the present day metropolis. On the waterfront with Lake Michigan, Chicago did not even have a breakwater. In fact, the first major dock for the harbor of Chicago was just being constructed in 1835 and the first light house had been established just three years earlier. One big problem troubling the port was that there was no way to get to the wannabe harbor. A hefty sandbar existed outside the harbor and there was no equipment anywhere in the region that could be used to dredge it. Arriving vessels had to unload their passengers into small yawl boats and row them ashore. Heavy cargo had to be lowered onto wooden rafts and then sculled ashore. Yet, even with its lack of accommodations, Chicago was fast becoming the gateway to the far west and a growing wave of pioneers were soon to force Chicago to grow into a key port city of the Great Lakes.

As the man history calls Elias Everett made his way along the waterfront, he was not just walking among the hub of the only transportation of the era, but also among the tools of communication. News from every town and village was transmitted by way of the lake and its vessel fleet. The telegraph, that in modern times we normally associate with communication back in the "olden days" was still years into the future. In fact, not far from that same Kingston waterfront, at New York University, in 1835 Samuel Morse had proved that signals could be transmitted by wire but was still two years from the birth of his telegraph system of communication which would one day outdate the movement of information by vessel. In the time of "Elias Everett," however, all communication was by word of mouth or written message carried by hand from place to place.

In the 1830s, it was then through the eastern lake ports of Buffalo and Kingston that the flood of immigrants and pioneers headed west flowed. Kingston itself had long been a primary seaport on Lake Ontario. Although some side-wheel steamers were making a good living on the lake, the primary source of water transportation was by sail and the Kingston waterfront was normally a forest of masts and rigging. Most of the wind-grabber captains scoffed openly at the big new steamers. After all, these new fangled steamboats were slow, awkward, and they had to be fed wood just to get underway. Sailing vessels were speedy, easily manipulated, and needed only God's wind to move along at twice the speed of a steamer. Add to that the fact that steamers had this nasty habit of blowing up and there was little to like about them - or so said the masters of the sail.

Steamers, however, had one advantage that sail powered boats could never match and that was comfort. In 1835, for the price of about $8, which would be the equivalent of $168 Canadian dollars in the year 2010, a passenger could buy a ticket on a steamer headed west which included stateroom plus the finest of meals and drinks all served by jacketed waiters. The most significant comfort that a person got on a steamer that they could not get on a wind-grabber, was warmth. The one thing that every steamer had plenty of was, of course, steam. That same steam could be piped into every room on the vessel. Such a comfort was something well appreciated on the Great Lakes where about two thirds of the sailing season is done in cold weather.

Of course, Mr. Everett's needs were such that he had no time to sit aboard a steamer while it went from port to port working its way toward his destination. Instead, he boarded his chartered, private, schooner and made his way to his berth. Captain Chandler eagerly welcomed him aboard. As best can be gleaned from the few records left to us, the date was November 10th, 1835, when the good captain ordered the lines of the *Robert Bruce* cast off and the little schooner set sail out of Kingston and, reported by one source, bound for "Hallowell," Ontario. One other source states that also aboard

13 HATS

the little schooner were three crewmen, their names recorded as Daniel Johnston, Albert Dye and someone by the name of Cook. Aboard *Bruce* there was no cargo, her only concern was her single passenger - the man history calls Elias Everett.

While the *Robert Bruce* made her way promptly from the harbor, her single passenger made himself comfortable in the boat's tiny cabin. He found a good place to hang coat and then he would have taken a moment to brush the waterfront's dust from his hat before hanging it up as well. This was an era when a man was easily judged by his hat, and there is no doubt that Elias Everett had a hat that was symbolic of who he was.

At about the same time as the *Robert Bruce* was getting under way headed westward, those passengers who were willing to sit aboard a steamer while it went from port to port working toward their particular destination, were crossing the gangplank to board the steamer *Cobourg* at her namesake port of Cobourg, Ontario. Unlike the *Robert Bruce*, the *Cobourg* would be headed east. Men were dressed in their finest wide lapelled coats and tails and topped with tall felt hats. Ladies were dressed in their best hooped skirts, gloves and frill. Cabin travel on a steamer was a formal occasion and everyone dressed properly. The ladies were escorted to the "ladies' cabin" by neatly uniformed cabin boys who struggled with their luggage. The ladies' cabin was on the uppermost deck and being 36 feet long, it had 16 berths. Gentlemen, meanwhile, were cabined on the next deck down in a cabin that was 90 feet long and had accommodations for 40 berths. The cabin boys who hauled the luggage to that deck could likely expect a fine tip of some sort of shiny coin. Such accommodations reflect the times, as this was an era when men traveled far more than ladies and in this class of passengers, children rarely came along.

Boarding the *Cobourg* on another gangplank was a different class of passengers, those who paid only for "deck" passage. Such passengers were largely immigrants or pioneers headed west. Such passage cost between $1 and $3 depending on the destination. In 2010 terms, that would be $21 and $56 Canadian. Such passage got the person nothing more than the privilege of standing, sitting and sleeping on the open deck. On some steamers a "forward deck" cabin was included to allow for shelter from the elements. That fore-deck area was divided into berths, but had no beds or furnishings of any sort. Deck passengers had to bring along their own provisions or would be sold meals and allowed to eat in a segregated dining room referred to as the "second table" which was normally out of the sight of the upper class passengers. Although such accommodations may sound crude by today's standards, in the 1800s it was actually the equivalent of taking your family on a trip and flying coach. Millions of people moved west in this manner, most carrying everything that they owned with them. And although the price may seem inexpensive by modern standards, consider that the same passage on a schooner could be bartered for little more than a nice fat goose.

Although we do not have an exact record of it in existence today, on the evening of November 10, 1835, the *Cobourg's* passenger list probably contained just a few "Deck" passengers and a modest load of "Cabin" passengers. She was headed eastbound for Kingston which was not the best direction to capture the immigrant passenger traffic. By 10:00 that evening, the boat's 21-foot diameter side wheels were digging into Lake Ontario in response to her two 50-horse-power low-pressure engines. Constructed just two years earlier, her hull measured 150 feet in keel length and she had a 25-foot beam. Under full steam the *Cobourg* could do a respectable 16-miles per hour or so boasted her owners. In command of the fine steamer stood Captain Paynter, who directed her steering pole out into the open expanse of Lake Ontario. If he had only known what had taken place over on Lake Michigan, Lake Huron and Lake Erie over the past day, he may have elected to stay in port. But, then again, this was the era of word of mouth and hand carried communications and so there was no way for Captain Paynter to know what was over his shoulder in the darkness of that autumn night. The lake, however, would soon come calling and, in fact, it would find the *Cobourg* in less than an hour.

Far to the west, on Lake Michigan, those unpopulated shores were now well populated with bodies and wrecked vessels. What had taken place was actually normal autumn weather, with blustery winds, rain and choppy seas being suddenly over-ridden by a very fast moving and extremely powerful sub-arctic, Canadian, low pressure system. In an era when captains relied almost totally on their experience and their barometers, both let them down. In this case, the barometer was already fairly low and the weather at the moment was in total agreement. So any captain would feel that he had a rough voyage ahead, but little to worry about. "The glass can't drop much farther" would have been the conclusion. That was absolutely wrong - the barometric pressure could drop farther - as a matter of fact it could drop a lot farther. It was simply the case that no captain on the lakes had ever seen it drop in the manner that it was about to. This would be the most powerful storm to sweep across the lakes in recorded history.

Instead of sweeping from northwest to east, southeast as most autumn gales do, the storm of 1835 came down from nearly due north. It hit upper Lake Michigan and northern Lake Huron first and every vessel with a yard of canvas out was an easy target. There was no large scale commerce working Lake Superior at this point in history with only the schooner *John Jacob Astor* plying Superior's waters. She was built in 1835 and there is no record of her being affected by the storm. On upper Lake Michigan, however, dozens of small schooners were scattered like leafs on a pond as the wind came thundering along. Many of these little vessels are not even in the records and it is conceivable that some could have simply been swallowed by the lake and completely lost to history. The *Lafayette*, however, did find her way into the records. With a load of flour and assorted merchandise, as well as several passengers aboard, she was blown ashore in the Straits of Mackinac. She was left there with a hole in her bottom, her cargo lost, but no reported loss of life.

Near Sleeping Bear point the schooner *Austerlitz* was blown ashore and wrecked. Prior to her fetching up there, Lake Michigan had taken pleasure in reaching aboard her and washing two passengers from her deck. Owned by Wisconsin fur trading magnate Michael Dousman, the *Austerlitz* was eventually recovered and returned to service. One source states that she was lost for the final time in 1836 and another states she was finished in 1844. One thing that we know for sure, however, is that Mr. Dousman's two passengers never made it past November 10, 1835.

Sweeping south, the storm hit the pocket of lower Lake Michigan and bottled up there, it found some easy victims. The schooner *Swan* was reportedly pounded down by the storm off of New Buffalo, Michigan - all aboard were lost to the lake. St. Joseph, Michigan, next became the recipient of the worst that the lake could serve. As evening set in, the 78-foot long schooner *Bridget* was hovering just outside the river off St. Joseph harbor. Captain Peter Duryea (also recorded as Drouillard) had previously stopped outside Chicago's sandbar and unloaded most of his passengers and cargo. They had also picked up two female missionaries bound for the Mackinaw wilderness. Now, he was poised to shuttle the remainder of his southbound passengers and freight into St. Joseph in a similar manner as had been done in Chicago, Lake Michigan, however, had other ideas.

Without warning, the storm came up and caught the *Bridget* in its clutches. The strongest winds that the Great Lakes had ever seen took hold of the schooner as the seas rapidly swelled into frightening peaks of ice water. The last that the people ashore saw of the *Bridget*, she was being blown helplessly away as her crew struggled to drop her anchor. She would later be found eight miles from the harbor, upside down and moored by that same anchor. Everyone aboard, including the captain's wife were gone, having been taken away forever by the lake.

It would be another 40 years before the United States Life-Saving Service would even begin to set up stations around the Great Lakes. So it was that with the wreck of the *Bridget* Lake Michigan was only beginning to deliver its load of sorrow onto the port village of St. Joseph and there would be no means of rescue for anyone. Through the night the storm howled and everyone ashore knew that it had caught many a vessel and many a soul off guard out on the lake. Those lucky enough to still be ashore were right, as somewhere north of St. Joseph the schooner *Chance* was beaten to death by the wind and seas. Early reports had her discovered off of St. Joseph at daylight with only her mast tops sticking above water. Later reports, however, stated that her overturned hull had come ashore at the same location. Considering that modern day divers have been actively searching for her and found nothing, it is unlikely that the masts sticking out of the water version of her discovery is the correct one. It is more than likely that she did wash ashore and perhaps went to pieces. In such a case, her hulk may have been dismantled or her remains scattered and buried in the sand. At any rate, the *Chance* and everyone aboard were swallowed by the lake.

Also being blown ashore at St. Joseph was the schooner *Llewellyn*. She came crashing into the mouth of the river around 3:00 in the morning. Unlike many in this story, both the *Llewellyn* and her crew would survive. The boat's cargo, however, would be a total loss.

South of St. Joseph the schooner *Utica* was thrown ashore by the gale. Her cargo of 200 barrels of salt was easily dissolved by the lake leaving only the empty barrels all over the beach. This time her people managed to survive after being beaten, soaked and benumbed by the frigid lake, but the *Utica* herself was a wreck. Some 40 miles south of St. Joseph the schooner *Marengo* was blown onto the beach - embarrassed, but uninjured just like her crew.

From the town of New Buffalo came the news that the schooner *Swan* had been lost with all hands just off shore and that cargo known to be aboard the schooner *Lodi* was coming onto the beaches. It was rumored that the *Lodi* had been lost with the *Swan*, but the *Lodi* eventually managed to limp into Grand River with her crew safe, but her deck-load missing.

Although this massive storm had raked Lake Michigan, at the same time its reach extended as far as Lake Erie and Lake Ontario. On Lake Erie the damage was mostly to property ashore. Water levels at Buffalo, although reported in some papers as having come up "20 feet" actually only came up two feet. Still that was significant rise in any gale.

At length, the monster storm swept across Lake Ontario, seeming to swallow the entire lake in a single gulp. Aboard the *Cobourg* the winds were felt to stiffen some 45 minutes after she entered the open lake. With a frightful speed, the power of the winds went from an autumn bluster to that of a fresh water hurricane. The steamer was just 10 miles out when Lake Ontario turned into an angry monster of cold death. Seas rapidly began to build against the steamer's beam and her passengers went from relaxing in comfort to holding on to whatever they could grip as the steamer started to roll.

Down below, the boat's engineer was fully occupied throttling her two engines as the boat rolled. Each roll would cause one of the boat's big paddle wheels to wallow deep into the water while the wheel on the opposite side would raise nearly out of the water and its engine would tend to race. This kept the engineer running from one engine to the other through the night. Of course, down in the dank, dark engine room, the time of the day was only known by the hands on the clock. Day or night, the engine room was only illuminated by a few dim oil lamps. The darkness was garnished by leaking steam and the odor of stacks of cordwood waiting to be added to the boiler's fire. Only the rolling of the deck beneath the engine room crew's feet hinted of the conditions topside.

Captain Paynter leaned out of the *Cobourg's* pilothouse window, took a sniff of the air and felt the buffet of the winds and instantly knew that his boat was in for some very bad weather. With that, he instantly put on his air of supreme, quiet confidence. Ordering the mate to hold her course, the good captain headed down to "visit" the passengers.

Steamer technology was still quite new in 1835 and as the master of one of those new-fangled vessels, Captain Paynter knew that he had to appear as calm as ice and solid in his confidence in his vessel. He had to show the passengers that he was unsinkable and therefore so may be the *Cobourg*. His outward calm and confidence would be infectious and no matter how bad the weather became, those passengers would carry in their minds the image of that rock-steady captain. If he kept the image up through the storm, then those passengers would spread the word that the *Cobourg* was rock-solid and as sturdy and safe as her captain. They would then be likely to book another trip and without doubt spread the word and cause others to book aboard the *Cobourg* as well.

So it was that Captain Paynter in his full uniform, polished brass buttons, mirror shined shoes and hat brim, strolled down into the parlors of the steamer *Cobourg*. All around him, there was commotion and an air of fear. As if casting a spell of calm, the good captain's presence, reassuring voice and demeanor of complete confidence simply wiped away the fear. Surrounded by porters cleaning up broken china slung from tables when the boat began to roll and passengers trying hard to simply remain seated or to stand, Captain Paynter stood ramrod straight, as if glued to the deck. Answering questions about the boat and the bad weather he calmed everyone with a simple answer of "She's well able" and "We are making good way." To everyone it seemed as if he had run the *Cobourg* through countless storms that were

13 HATS

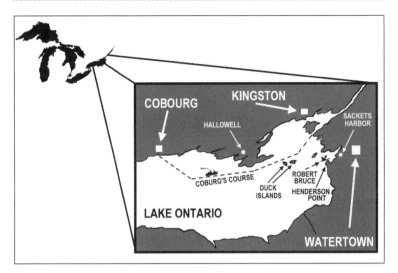

worse than this one. Indeed he was a steamboat master and he had every inch of this new, huge, machine under his total control. As the good captain excused himself and headed back to the pilothouse following his visit, he also had the passengers well under his control.

Facing a quartering wind out of the northeast, the *Cobourg* wallowed ahead in the storm until three o'clock that morning. It was then that the wind suddenly died. To some this may have led to the assumption that the storm was over. To an experienced mariner, however, a wind that dies suddenly in a gale means that very bad things are soon coming. Captain Paynter told his crew to watch out of the nor'west. There was no sense tapping the glass, he told them. "It's as low as its going to go tonight." He was right. Just before four o'clock the wind exploded from out of the northwest.

Spitting snow and ripping the crests from the waves, the wind caught the *Cobourg* in the upper east end of Lake Ontario just west of the Duck Islands. Now the waves that had been running from the northeast met the wind angled against them. Worse yet, this northwest wind was making its own waves that were bouncing off the eastern shore of Lake Ontario and running back toward the west. All of this brewed up a confused sea where the huge waves simply formed pinnacles of ice water that leaped from the surface and then collapsed back into the lake. This action caused the *Cobourg* to corkscrew and to roll wildly. Now the water came aboard and danced gleefully on the steamer's decks. Cascades of water burst cabin windows and smashed in doors. Carpets in the parlors were awash as tables and chairs were rearranged by Lake Ontario into a constantly shifting pattern of chaos.

Daylight found the *Cobourg* rolling drunkenly as her bow spent more time under the water than above it. Still, when the mate came up from below decks he reported that very little water was coming in and the boat's pumps were easily handling it. Captain Paynter's boat appeared to be weathering the storm with only minor fuss. For other mariners, however, the story was very different. From the *Cobourg's* pilothouse window the sight of a small schooner capsized by the storm came into view among the heaving seas. Clinging to the boat's keel were two people and one of them was waving a cloth in an attempt to signal the *Cobourg*. In the confused seas, there was not a chance that the big steamer could get anywhere near the little boat and so Captain Paynter had no choice other than to continue on and leave the poor souls to their fate at the frigid hands of Lake Ontario. When the *Cobourg* was about two miles from the Duck Islands another small overturned schooner was sighted. Mercifully, this time there was no sign of life on or near the wreck. Captain Paynter and the pilothouse crew of the *Cobourg* stood in silence, gazing from the spray spattered windows and wondering what additional horrors may lay ahead. With that single thought haunting them, the crew of the *Cobourg* pressed on toward Kingston.

13 HATS

By nine o'clock that morning, the *Cobourg* was abeam of Kingston where she was supposed to land 3 cabin passengers and 15 deck passengers. So rough were the seas, however, that there was simply no way that Captain Paynter could risk turning the steamer. Instead, he was compelled to run for the shelter of the St. Lawrence River and his terminal destination of Prescott, Ontario. His Kingston passengers would simply have to remain aboard and be dropped off during the trip back.

Perhaps with an indiscernible sigh of relief from her stalwart master, the steamer *Cobourg* rolled into the confines of the St. Lawrence that afternoon. She had gotten a good wetting from the lake and her crew, including her captain, had gotten a reminder of their own mortality. No one in that pilothouse would ever forget the image of those stranded men clinging to the keel of that little schooner and left to find their doom out on the lake.

Two days after the storm the remains of the little schooner *Robert Bruce* washed ashore on Henderson Point in northern Mexico Bay. Although Lake Ontario had stripped the little schooner of every soul onboard, it did not loot the vessel completely. Inside the schooner's deckhouse was found a single jacket hanging on a nail. In it was $719 and "papers" belonging to Elias Everett. From that finding, it was concluded and universally reported that a man named Elias Everett, of Watertown, New York, was lost aboard the *Robert Bruce* on November 10th, 1835. But, with that report is seeded the puzzle of Elias Everett.

In looking more closely at this story a number of questions pop up. This is because the facts surrounding the passenger of the *Robert Bruce* and the man who was Elias Everett tend not to line up nor add up. First of all, genealogical research finds that in 1835 there was an Elias Everett who lived in Watertown. That city was a good sized community of nearly

5,000 people established in Jefferson County, New York. There are, however, no birth or death dates recorded for this person, which is not unusual for the early 1800s. He was a farmer and owned 300 acres of land, or a bit less than one half square mile. The other members of the Everett family lived near one another and were primarily farmers. The single exception was Elias' older brother Austin, who served as under-Sheriff. Overall, these people held land large enough to feed their families and to do some limited local trading, they were not wealthy people. So, what would Elias Everett be doing all the way over in Canada, chartering a private schooner with such a huge sum of cash in his possession? Watertown is about 18 miles from Sackets Harbor, the nearest Lake Ontario port. That route was, in 1835, a full day's journey by horse and wagon over a "road" that was little more than a dirt trail.

To equate this into 2010 terms, this would be like a man who owns a farm of about two square miles near his extended family in South Carolina being killed in the crash of a private jet that he chartered to fly him from Vancouver to Moose Jaw and having $15,000 in cash in his possession. There is almost no reason for such circumstances to develop in 2010 and even less reason in 1835.

The next question is, if the man in our story actually was Elias Everett, how did this simple farmer end up with $719 in his possession? Although some people, such as the captains of the largest lake steamboats, could have annual earnings of a similar amount in 1835, this amount is far, far beyond anything that a farmer owning 300 acres could even imagine.

Another question is what sort of business would draw a farmer such as Elias Everett from his homestead and see him traveling from Kingston to Hallowell? Farmers have always tended to stick very close to their own land. So, it seems

13 HATS

against the nature of most farmers to adventure away from the daily chores that their land requires.

Lastly, there is the fact that, as of this writing, no grave can be found for Elias Everett. Although this is not unusual considering that many simple folks were buried on their own land with simple, wooden markers which were easily erased by the passage of time, it could also mean that there is no grave, because there was no body. Elias Everett may have indeed been swallowed by Lake Ontario and is now resting with tens of thousands of others lost forever on the Great Lakes.

With all of that in mind we can now review several possibilities. The most compelling of these involves the subject of finance and how money was handled in the early 1800s. Much like today, many municipal and private ventures were financed my large banks in metropolitan areas such as Boston, New York, or even Kingston. Application for such finance, as well as the monies involved, were moved, like everything else in 1835, by hand. Couriers would be hired to carry both cash and paperwork to and from the different parties involved in the transaction. Thus, for example, to finance something such as a new bridge, the town fathers would apply to a bank by sending a courier to that bank. The bank would consider the request and send written terms, by courier, back to the municipality. If the terms were agreed upon, the borrower would send a courier back to the lender and that courier would later return with the cash. Once the project was finished, the borrower would gather the cash needed to pay off the loan and send a courier with the cash back to the bank before the due date to pay off the note. Anyone considered to have a local reputation as being "reliable" could be hired as a courier.

It so happens that the village of Watertown was in a building boom between 1833 and 1836. Several wool mills,

ALL HANDS ON DECK

tanning mills and a water lime factory were being built. Additionally, a wooden covered bridge was constructed over the Black River that ran through Watertown. All of those projects had to be financed and much of that cash had to come from banks outside of Watertown. That cash was carried in large disbursements by couriers. Such disbursements were likely in the form of structured payouts rather than a single lump sum. If we consider that single-source's report that stated that Hallowell was the *Robert Bruce's* destination to be wrong and instead interpolate the schooner's destination as being Sackets Harbor it would make a course that would be consistent with where she was washed up after the storm. In those circumstances we can offer up the supposition that perhaps farmer Elias Everett, his planting, growing and harvest seasons being over for the year, decided to earn some extra income by acting as a courier. With a nine-year-old son, William, and a four-year-old daughter, Pamela, at home and a long cold winter ahead, the extra income could do the family a lot of good. A city-paid trip to Kingston and back could be a far easier way to earn money than plowing fields. It is also stated that along with the bundle of $719 in cash, some "important papers" were found in the jacket said to belong to Elias Everett. All of this begins to add up to the job of a courier.

Of course there is also the possibility that the person who was aboard the *Robert Bruce* was not Elias Everett at all. It may be that the man had in his jacket some papers with nothing more than Elias Everett's name upon them. We have to keep in mind that these papers had been soaked by the lake for several days and may have been discovered by persons who were either illiterate or only semi-literate. Illiteracy was wide-spread in the early 1800s and it is easy to picture a scenario where a few people find water-soaked papers and only the name "Elias," or "Everett" or some similar names can be recognized along with the name "Watertown." When that word gets back to the local newspapers it is morphed into Elias Everett of Watertown being lost aboard the *Robert Bruce* when, in fact, he is alive and well, working in his barn and waiting for his papers to be delivered.

There is also the remote chance that the man on the *Robert Bruce* was a different Elias Everett who had business in Hallowell and never intended to go near Watertown. When the wreck of the *Robert Bruce* washed up on Henderson Point, the people who discovered the cash and papers saw the name and, because of proximity alone, simply associated it as being the person who lived in nearby Watertown. That word was passed to the news media and spread far and wide as fact.

A solution to the puzzle that is the enigma of Elias Everett and his $719 could be as close as a modern visit to Watertown or as distant as November 11th, 1835. As of this writing I leave it up to you, the reader, to ponder from now on. I've been pondering it for over two years now and what you read here is what I have. One additional detail I can add is that the same team that found the *Robert Bruce's* remains also found a total of 13 hats washed up on the beach. There were hats of mariners, hats of laborers, hats of farmers, hats of gentlemen, hats of couriers and hats of business men. The biggest question left to us by history is - which hat did Elias Everett wear?

GLOSSARY

Abeam - Directly beside a vessel

Aft - Toward the rear of a vessel

Back - A ship's spine or keel

Barge - A vessel that has no power of its own and must be towed

Beam - The width of a vessel

Beam Ends - The sides of a vessel

Boat - On the great lakes, a ship is called a boat

Bulkhead - A wall-like partition that divides a boat's hull

Bunker - A compartment where a boat's fuel is stored

Capstan - Device used for pulling lines or chains

Firehold - The part of the engine room where the boiler fires are fed

Fo'c'sle - The raised part of a boat's bow containing crew quarters

Founder - To sink in a disastrous way

Funnel - A steamer's smokestack

Hawser - A tow line, steel or rope

Heel - To lean to one side

Keel - A supporting beam that runs the length of a boat's bottom

List - A tilt to one side

ALL HANDS ON DECK

Lighter - To raise a sunken boat by removing its cargo

Port Side - Left side

Saltie - An ocean going vessel that visits the lakes

Schooner-barge - A sailing vessel that is usually towed

Screw - Propeller

Spardeck - The maindeck through which cargo is loaded

Texas Deck - The deck atop which the pilothouse is mounted

Yawl - A small rowboat or lifeboat

REFERENCES

THEY WERE WRONG

Fond du Lac Reporter, 10/31/1887, 11/1,2,3,5/1887
Marquette Daily Mining Journal, 10/31/1887,
11/1,2,3,4,5,8/1887
Chicago Inter Ocean, 10/31/1887
Kingston Daily British Whig, 10/27,31/1887, 11/3,4,5,7/1887
Bay City Tribune, 10/30/1887, 11/1,3,5,8,9/1887
Saginaw Courier, 11/2,5/1887
Chicago Tribune, 10/30/1887, 11/12/1887
Wauseon Northwestern Republican, 11/4/1887
Annual Report of the United States Life-Saving Service, 1888
Lake Superior Shipwrecks - Wolf
Images of America, Maritime Chicago-Karamanski, Tank
"The Tragic Loss of the Propeller *Vernon*" *Anchor News*, July-August 1979: Hirthe et.al.
National Archives, Washington DC - vessel information reply
Polk Marine Directory, 1883
Vernon Master Sheet: Institute for Great Lakes Research
Bowling Green Historical collection - online vessel index, *S.B. Pomeroy*
Marine Record 11/3/1887

COPS... IN OSWEGO

Oswego Commercial Times, 5/22/1860
The Democracy (Buffalo NY), 4/25/1855
Toronto Globe, 10/24/1856, 10/29/1861

Buffalo Commercial Advertiser, 10/27,28/1861
Vincent's semi-annual United States Register, January-July 1860
Great Lakes Shipwreck File, Swayze
E-mail correspondence from Richard Palmer, 10/6/2000
"The Bay of Dead Ships," Reich
"Images of America - Around Oswego," Prior, Siembor
"History of the Great Lakes," Beers
"Lake Ontario," Pound

THE RITES OF SPRING

Namesakes, 1900-1909, 1910-1919, Greenwood
Namesakes II, Greenwood
Marine Review, 9/19, 26/1895, 5/7/1896, 1/5/1899, 5/4, 18, 25/1899
Marine Record, 9/5/1895, 5/6/1897
Great Lakes Ships We Remember, Vol. I & II, Van der Linden
Detroit Free Press, 9/1/1895
Sault Saint Marie Evening News, 4/19, 21, 24, 26, 28, 30/1909; 5/1, 4/1909
The Telescope, May-June 1992, A Classic Class Part III, Dewar
Freshwater Whales, Wright
Beeson's Marine Directory, 1910
Maritime History of the Great Lakes website
Phone conversation with Tom Farnquist, 8/3/1992

AX MEN

Ashtabula Weekly Telegraph, 11/14,21/1879
USLSS Annual Report, 1880
Great Lakes Shipwreck File, Swayze
"Wreck Ashore," Stonehouse
"Log Marks," Thornton
"Michigan Places and Names," Romig

REFERENCES

"History of the Great Lakes", Beers
"Lake Huron," Landon
"List of Merchant Vessels of the United States," 1884

SOMETIMES YOU JUST HAVE TO WAIT YOUR TURN

USLSS Annual Report, 1887
Merchant Vessel List, 1889
Buffalo Commercial Advertiser, 5/13/1874
The Marine Record, 4/7/1887, 12/8/1887
Great Lakes Shipwreck File, Swayze
"Wreck Ashore," Stonehouse
"Fathoms Deep But Not Forgotten: Wisconsin's Lost Ships Vol. I," Baillod
"Scow Schooners of San Francisco Bay," Olmsted
"Namesakes 1920-1929," Greenwood
"History of the Great Lakes," Beers
"Lake Huron," Landon
"List of Merchant Vessels of the United States," 1884

Little Lady of the Lakes

Petoskey News-Review, 5/22/2010
Boatnerd.com, 5/23/2010
E-mail correspondence with LT Cory D. Cichoracki, 6/4/2010, 8/18/2010, 10/12/2010

ALONG PRIDGEON'S LINE

Saginaw Daily Courier, 9/12/1875
Cleveland Newspaper Digest, Jan. to Dec. 1859
Chicago Inter Ocean, 9/20, 22/1875
Chicago Tribune, 4/12,14/1869
Port Huron Daily Times, 9/14,16/1875
Toronto Daily Globe, 9/15,16,17,18/1875

ALL HANDS ON DECK

Amherstburg Echo, 9/17/1875

Buffalo Commercial Advertiser, 1/28/1858, 2/26/1867, 10/23/1870, 11/17/1880

Toronto Globe, 9/17/1875

List of Merchant Vessels of the United States, 1874, 1884

Lake Underwriters Classification, 1871, 1873, 1875

Great Lakes Shipwreck File, Swayze

Phone conversation with Rod Danielson of Rods Reef Diving, Ludington, MI, 3/31/1992

Card catalog of the Great Lakes Historical Society, Vermillion, OH, 2/21/92

"Around the Lakes," 1894, Detroit Dry Dock Company

"Freshwater Whales," Wright

"Namesakes 1900-09," Greenwood

"Ice Water Museum," Oleszewski

"History of the Great Lakes," Beers

"List of Merchant Vessels of the United States," 1884

"Blue Book of American Shipping," 1897

THE BEST LAID PLANS OF CHARLES EVANS

Port Huron Weekly Times, 12/2/1870

Port Huron Daily Times, 11/2/1878

Chicago Inter Ocean, 11/4,11,14,20,26/1878

Detroit Post & Tribune, 11/8, 16,20,21/1878

Daily News (Kingston), 11/26,29/1870

Detroit Free Press, 3/29/1871

Classification of Vessels, 1871

Great Lakes Shipwreck File, Swayze

Maritime History of the Great Lakes website

Marine Disasters of the Western Lakes, 1869, 1871, Hall

REFERENCES

CHRISTENED WITH WATER - INTERRED WITH DYNAMITE

Port Huron Weekly Times, 4/27/1871, 5/4,25/1871, 6/1/71
Port Huron Daily Times, 11/25/1870
Port Huron Times, 5/4/1871, 6/3/1871
Detroit Free Press, 4/16,25/1871, 9/19/1900
Buffalo Morning Express, 6/9/1871
Buffalo Evening News, 10/21,22,25/1905, 7/19/1906
"List of Merchant Vessels of the United States," 1884, 1892
Detroit Post & Tribune, 8/30/1882
Marine Record, 7/7/1887
"Vessels Built on the Saginaw," Swayze, Roberts, Comtois
"Davidson's Goliaths," Cooper, Jensen
"Dive Ontario" Kohl

FIRST OF THE DOOMED SISTERS

Bay City Times-Press, 10/26,27,28,29/1898
"Ghost Ships of the Great Lakes," Boyer
"Great Lakes Ships We Remember" Vol. I, II,III, Van der Linden
"Fathoms Deep But Not Forgotten: Wisconsin's Lost Ships Vol. I," Baillod
"Stormy Seas," Oleszewski
"Stormy Disasters," Oleszewski
"Know Your Ships 2009," LaLievre
Brendon Baillod's web site: www.ship-wreck.com
E-mail correspondence with Brendon Baillod, 6/28/2010, 7/7,8,9/2010, 8/19,23,24/2010

A PEEK INSIDE THE BLODGETT FLEET

Letter from Omer William Blodgett, undated.
Phone conversation with Don Comtois, Bay City maritime historian, 10/31/2010
Marine Review, Feb., 1906

"Lake Superior Shipwrecks," Wolff
"Namesakes 1930-1955," Greenwood
"Namesakes 1920-1929," Greenwood
"Vessels Built on the Saginaw," Swayze, Roberts, Comtois
Walter Lewis: Maritime History of the Great Lakes web site
Historical Collection of the Great Lakes Vessel Index
Transcription by Teresa Oleszewski

13 HATS

Kingston Chronicle & Gazette, 11/16/1833, 4/5/1834, 10/4/1834,
3/11/1835, 7/5/1834, 4/29/1835, 5/9/1835,
11/14,18,21,25,28/1835, 12/2/1835
Oswego Palladium, 5/14/1834, 11/18,25/1835
Chicago Democrat, 11/18,25/1835
Buffalo Whig & Journal, 11/18,25/1835, 12/9/1835
Niles (Michigan) Gazette and Advertiser, 11/21/1835
Detroit Democratic Free Press, 12/7/1835
Dave Swayze: Great Lakes Shipwreck File
"History of the Great Lakes," Beers
"History of Jefferson County in the State of New York from the
Earliest Period to the Present Time," Hough, Sterling and Riddell
"150 Years of Watertown: A History," Landon
Walter Lewis: Maritime History of the Great Lakes web site
Conversation with historical preservationist Craig Oleszewski,
Architectural Conservator/Exhibits Specialist
Brendon Baillod - Paper from NASOH Conference, Manitowoc,
WI, 05/01/2006
Phone Conversation with Terry Namdigo, Flower Memorial Library Genealogy Department, 6/29/2010
Multiple e-mails from genealogist Kristi Robins 6/29,30/2010

ABOUT THE AUTHOR

Author W. Wes Oleszewski was born and raised in mid-Michigan and spent most of his life with an eye turned toward the Great Lakes. Since 1991 he has authored 14 books on the subject of Great Lakes maritime history and lighthouses.

Noted for his meticulous research, Oleszewski has a knack for weeding out the greatest of details from the most obscure events and then weaving those facts into the historical narratives which are his stories. His tales of actual events are real enough to thrill any reader while every story is technically correct and highly educational. Oleszewski feels that the only way to teach history in this age of computer and video games is through "narrative." The final product of his efforts are captivating books that can be comfortably read and enjoyed by everyone from the eldest grandmother to the grade-school kid and future historian.

Born on the east side of Saginaw, Michigan, in 1957, Wes Oleszewski attended public school in that city through grade nine, when his family moved to the town of Freeland, Michigan. In 1976 he graduated from Freeland High School and a year later entered the Embry-Riddle Aeronautical University in Daytona, Florida. Working his way through college by way of his own earned income alone, Oleszewski graduated in 1988 with a commercial pilot's certificate, "multi-engine and instrument airplane" ratings as well as a B.S. Degree in Aeronautical Science. Along with his writing, he has pursued a career as a professional pilot. He holds an A.T.P. certificate and to date has logged thousands hours of flight time, most of which is in airline category and jet aircraft. Currently, he works as a writer and editorial cartoonist. He is married and has two daughters.